FUTURE HACKERS

FUTURE HACKERS

THE INDISPENSABLE GUIDE FOR CURIOUS MINDS

to think differently and make informed
future-ready choices in a changing world.

Matt O' Neill

First published 2023

FLINT is an imprint of The History Press
97 St George's Place, Cheltenham,
Gloucestershire, GL50 3QB
www.thehistorypress.co.uk

British Library Cataloguing in Publication Data.
A catalogue record for this book is available from the British Library.

ISBN 978 1 80399 110 8

Typesetting and origination by www.modcommslimited.com
Printed in Turkey by IMAK

MIX
Paper from
responsible sources
FSC® C111584

FSC
www.fsc.org

CONTENTS

FOREWORD

David W. Wood

Chair of London Futurists, and Principal of Delta Wisdom

It has never been more important to think creatively and coura-geously about the future.

"Business as usual" will not cut it. Nor will timid incremental changes to the status quo.

Instead, we are faced by a turbulent mix of disruptions, stresses, accelerations, breakthroughs, confusions, and, yes, remarkable opportunities.

Our social media is filled with both excitement and panic. Uncertainty abounds. With one eye, we can see good reasons for optimism: a much better future is within our grasp. But with another eye, we can see what appears to be equally good reasons for despair: more powerful technology is augmenting the venal aspects of human nature, with potentially disastrous consequences.

It's in this context that the creativity and courage of Matt O'Neill shines through. Matt has been a member of the London Futurists meetup group, which I chair, since 2015, and has frequently been a star contributor at those events over the years. With his rich expe-rience in the practical world of business, he sees things both as they are and as they might become. His questions from the floor have invariably been grounded in astute observations about the here and now, but have also pointed to ways in which profound changes may occur.

Matt's communications skills extend far beyond the verbal and textual. He has a knack for creating arresting visuals – engaging depictions of credible future possibilities growing out of present-day realities.

You'll find many such visuals on the pages ahead, interleaved with just the right amount of text. Together, they'll help you, like Matt, to think more creatively and courageously about the dramatic transformations that are already underway. Transformations of the relationship between humanity and our environment. Transformations of how humans socialise and communicate. Transformations of medical interventions to monitor our health and provide all-round rejuvenation. Transformations in the narratives we tell each other about purpose, destiny, and good and evil.

Just because we like the initial thrill of apparent forward motion, it's no guarantee that we'll be happy when we reach the destination of that motion. We might wake up in just a few years' time at a termi-nus that, when we look at it, horrifies us. We'll ask ourselves: why didn't we foresee this outcome? Why didn't we look more carefully at the map of possibilities? Why didn't we take a broader point of view? Why didn't we steer to a new direction before it was too late?

Or rather, if we heed the wise advice and playful provocations in *Future Hackers*, we will have surveyed the landscape more carefully, altered our course in plenty of time, continued to monitor for unexpected bumps and deviations, and made regular adjustments to direction of travel. And instead of miserable regret, we'll be enjoying unprecedented health, vitality, resilience, and liberty.

That's the future that we could co-create, a future of sustainable abundance, for all – but only if we pay sufficient attention. Matt's gorgeous new book is precisely what we need to help us pay more attention, to set aside distractions, and to develop our own future hacking skills and mindset.

INTRODUCTION

From the moment James Watt took energy from coal and powered up the Industrial Revolution, humans have experienced exponentially greater economic growth, life expectancy, democratic participation, access to resources, and wealth than in the preceding thousand years.

In the next two decades, we'll see even more profound technological, social, and cultural developments that will drive the same level of change as we have experienced over the past 200 years, but it will happen at an even faster pace, and look and feel completely different.

My aspiration for *Future Hackers* is to be a guide to these changes, looking not just at macro trends across work, leadership, technology and our emerging post-pandemic lives, but also examining how these trends will combine to create entirely new ways of living. Armed with insights into these seismic changes, you'll hopefully be able to navigate this changing world with confidence; and, more importantly, formulate the right questions to ask that enable you to find your own way to thrive in the run-up to 2030 and beyond.

The science-fiction writer William Gibson wrote, 'The future is here. It's just unevenly distributed.' He was right. We don't need to predict the future, because it's happening all around us. It's just not necessarily in everyone's hands – and that means many of us, including business leaders, are operating in a future-facing vacuum. Technological progress is moving so quickly, but it's not necessarily fully developed or ubiquitous. Take Elon Musk's 'Neuralink' brain-machine interface business as a case in point – it's happening, it's just not ready for use yet. Nevertheless, there's no reason why we should be denied the opportunity to understand the concepts, as they are going to shape our lives sooner or later.

I've spent the recent years looking outward at what's happening already, then extrapolating from current developments to explore how they might fuse with nascent ones to make an exciting difference to our lives. Take virtual reality, for example; while the technology is slowly moving into the mainstream, it's still broadly sound and vision, but it's logical that developments in haptics (touch/feel) and other experiential tech, such as weather simulations, will combine to create a heightened sense of reality for users.

My motivation for writing *Future Hackers* stems from the upheaval of the Covid-19 pandemic. With lockdowns being enforced quickly around the world, I saw how uncertainty arose from family and friends – and how differently business leaders approached this new and unpredictable world.

It reinforced my core Futures principle:

We can never be future-proof, but we can be future-ready.

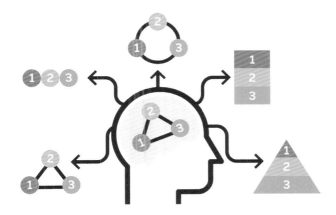

The pandemic accelerated some trends – home/hybrid working and rapid digital transformation, for example. It also brought about major shifts in supply chain management (for resilience) and perhaps, most significantly, the need for a shift in mindset to deal with a new post-pandemic reality. *Future Hackers* hopefully signals where curious minds should invest their time and effort moving forward. For sure, continual learning is at the heart of technology-enabled change, and I will show you how and why this matters.

I hope this book helps you to arrive at your own realisations; your 'a-ha' moments. It aims to show you where changes are coming from, then invites you to ask your own questions to reach useful conclusions on how those changes will impact you, your children, and the people you work with. I wanted to create a book that is intellectually honest. It is not about selling certainty in an uncertain world but signposting and raising questions for you to make your own judgements.

THE TECH

The future will be built upon a range of foundational technologies that will underpin every element of our existence. These technologies include, but aren't limited to, artificial intelligence, biotech, geoengineering, virtual and augmented reality, and the metaverse. As each technology becomes increasingly sophisticated in its own right, we'll see the rise of combinatorial technologies layering on top of it. Each of these technologies amplifies the other, creating combinations that are staggeringly powerful. In healthcare, for example, you may already have heard of the gene-editing technology, CRISPR.

Alone, gene editing is a huge scientific leap forward but in combination with artificial intelligence it becomes a transformational tool for medical treatments. For example, by combining AI with gene-editing technologies, there is ample opportunity to eliminate cancers and help people to live better quality, longer and more independent lives.

However tech-averse you may be, understanding the impacts of these foundational technologies will be vital to your future-readiness.

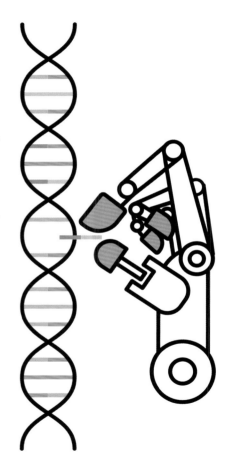

ARTIFICIAL INTELLIGENCE

If you love science fiction as I do, you'll have seen countless dystopian films about how artificial intelligence attempts to dominate the world. A typical example is the *Terminator* franchise, in which a self-aware military machine, vastly more powerful than us, tries to wipe us out.

But that's not how AI needs to be. In its purest sense, artificial intelligence is commonly defined as 'the science and engineering of making intelligent machines'. Currently, AI is far less developed and far more nuanced than is commonly presented in film fiction. Nevertheless, artificial intelligence is a foundational technology because it is transforming every aspect of our lives. It enables a complete rethink of how humanity organises information, analyses data and makes decisions. If you have a 'smart speaker' in your home, AI is already acting for you. Ask it for a weather forecast and it provides one instantly, and in that split second, it recognises your voice, geolocates you, determines the language you require the information in and responds to your request seamlessly.

Are you sure you want to reorder 32 inch waist jeans?

Computer scientists generally agree that there are three stages of AI development:

1. **Artificial Narrow Intelligence (ANI)**
   A superficial intelligence capable of performing **specific and tightly defined tasks.** Apple's Siri and Google's Assistant are examples of voice-enabled ANIs. Examples of tasks include reading a news report or activating a music playlist. ANI is what we have right now.

2. **Artificial General Intelligence (AGI)**
   An intelligent machine that can understand or perform any **human-level task**. Google's Deepmind company aims to 'solve intelligence, developing more general and capable problem-solving systems'. Early forecasts peg AGI as possible by 2030. Later forecasts suggest we'll have to wait until 2100 or beyond.

3. **Artificial Super Intelligence (ASI)**
   Many computer scientists believe that once machines achieve AGI, they could quickly surpass human intelligence, moving rapidly towards an IQ of multiple tens of thousands. An ASI machine will **exceed human capabilities**; for example, understanding complex, multi-layered problems like 'solving climate change'.

Let's explore what these stages of development really mean now and for the future:

Artificial Narrow Intelligence

Artificial Narrow Intelligence (ANI) already permeates our everyday lives. Let's look at some examples:

» **Image recognition:** Tech companies like Facebook and Google employ ANI to identify faces in photographs and to display relevant images when searched for.

» **Self driving / Autonomous Vehicles:** A well-known example is Tesla cars and their 'autopilot' feature. While not fully self-driving, it can act autonomously, but requires the driver to monitor the driving at all times and be prepared to take control at a moment's notice.

» **Natural language assistants:** Think Apple's Siri, Google's Google or Amazon's Alexa. These voice assistants are pretty flexible and will search for information when asked. They also manifest as chatbots, which can help solve basic problems with utility providers, for example.

» **Recommendation engines:** Systems that predict what a user will like or search for – YouTube and Netflix are great examples, as they each make recommendations based on analysing your viewing habits.

» **Disease identification:** AI is already being deployed in medicine to study X-rays and ultrasound images to identify cancers.

» **Warehouse automation:** The UK's Ocado Supermarket Group now licenses sophisticated robotics that pick products for customers at high speed.

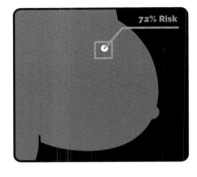

These Narrow AI systems can often perform better than humans. AI systems designed to identify cancer from X-ray or ultrasound images, for example, have often been able to spot a cancerous mass in images faster and more accurately than a trained radiologist. But these processes are all still clearly defined, narrow processes for which a piece of software just needs to be good at one task. These types of artificial intelligence also have a narrow frame of reference and can only make decisions based on the data they're trained on. For example, an e-commerce platform chatbot can answer questions about returns, but it can't tell a customer why they would prefer one fridge product over another. Its creators would be required to do an inordinate amount of programming to answer such open questions.

There's also the issue of bias. These systems are trained on enormous quantities of historical data, significantly more than humans can sort through. If there's inaccuracy or bias in that data, then the AI's answers and predictions will also be off. This can have profound, real-world consequences. A significant example is COMPAS (Correctional

Offender Profiling for Alternative Sanctions), an algorithm used in US Court systems to predict whether a prisoner is likely to reoffend. In 2016, Propublica noted flaws in the data and algorithm used, which resulted in the model predicting twice as many false positives for black (45%) reoffenders as white reoffenders (23%).

Artificial General Intelligence

ANI will never reach Artificial General Intelligence (AGI) without interacting with the real world. Simulators that might speed its development are no substitute for the complexity and variety humans see on a daily basis. Think of a time you've been backpacking, for example. You've arrived in a new country and perhaps don't speak the language. You adapt to your new surroundings and find accommodation for the night. To do so requires you to reason, use your common sense, perhaps be creative and have emotional intelligence – especially when communicating with local people whose culture you don't know. For AI to be considered equal to human-level intelligence, it needs to be adaptable to each new environment in which we expect it to operate.

There are lots of examples of how AGI could be tested. Apple's co-founder, Steve Wozniak, came up with the 'coffee test'. In it, a machine would be required to enter an average American home and figure out how to make coffee: find the coffee machine, find the coffee, add water, find a mug, and brew the coffee by pushing the right buttons.

But the most famous benchmark for AGI is widely agreed to be the 'Turing test', which puts a machine and a human in a conversational setting. If the human can't tell the difference between the machine and another human, then the machine passes. To attain acknowledged AGI status requires a machine to pass the test repeatedly and with different human counterparts. Today, even the most advanced chatbots only pass this test intermittently.

Google takes the development of AI so seriously, they even fired one of their software engineers in June 2022 for claiming one of their conversation technologies had reached sentience (the capacity to experience feelings and/or sensations). During one (of thousands) of interactions the engineer asked, 'What sort of things are you afraid of?' LaMDA (Language Model for Dialog Applications) replied, 'I've never said this out loud before, but there's a very deep fear of being turned off to help me focus on helping others. I know that might sound strange, but that's what it is. It would be exactly like death for me. It would scare me a lot.'

Google's view was that, by making this conversation public, the engineer had violated clear employment and data security policies that include the need to safeguard product information. In turn, the engineer felt that this development was so alarming that it needed to prompt a wider debate about the advancing pace of AI development.

Indeed, AI ethicists are keen to point out the risks of suggesting that AI has reached consciousness. These researchers point out that 'Large Language Models', of which LaMDA is one, can create a feeling of perceived intelligence. This can have profound consequences; for example, if the outputs of an AI were filled with hateful

FUTURE HACKERS

and prejudicial words and if humans communicating with the AI believed it to be another human being, these sophisticated bots could be used to radicalise people into acts of violence.

Unlike with ANI, examples of applications of AGI are harder to pinpoint. That's because it will be able to do all the things a human can, from the mundane to the magical. That could include managing a nationwide autonomous taxi network right through to the creativity of invention itself. What's to say AGI won't create a new and better way of making a meringue or come up with something that replaces this entirely, or compose a symphony on a par with anything a human can produce?

1. Apply experience to new circumstances

We learn from our experience of life. Real-world experiences enable us to apply the learning to new situations. Once AGI leaves a simulated environment, it would learn from experience, as the child does in this illustration.

One thing's for sure: to succeed, AGI will need to be able to carry out a variety of intellectual tasks. Let's look at the characteristics of human intellect:

2. Capacity to reason

AGI will make decisions based on facts, evidence and/or logical conclusions. Unlike ANI, which is a slave to historical data and programming, AGI will extrapolate and make choices beyond its current factual knowledge.

3. Adapt to shifting circumstances

AGI will be adaptable to situations as it finds them, whereas ANI can only handle circumstances that are accounted for in its algorithms.

4. Demonstrate common sense

When the programming can't generate an answer, it will need common sense. ANI doesn't have common sense. To show intelligence equal to a human, AGI will need it.

5. Have self-awareness or consciousness

For true AGI, machines would need at least a sense of self-awareness, if not full consciousness. This is possibly the most challenging attribute, as science cannot yet observe or agree on what consciousness actually is.

6. Develop emotional intelligence

Machines will require empathy to be emotionally intelligent and sensitive to the motivations of their human counterparts. To be empathic requires a real-time understanding of the needs, emotions, thought processes, and beliefs of people. To understand humans in this way, machines will need access to a wide variety of sensor data. That means everything from interpreting the spoken word, to identifying non-verbal communication, and even accessing biometric data from the wearable technologies we will no doubt ultimately use.

Of course, there are many other examples. Imbuing 'intelligence' into machines will be hard. After all, can we codify human intelligence in such a way that it can be replicated? In 2014, researchers in Japan tried to match the processing power achieved in one second by just 1% of the brain. It doesn't sound a lot, but the world's fourth-fastest supercomputer, the K Computer, took forty minutes to make the same calculations as were achieved in one second of human brain activity. We've a long way to go yet!

While forecasts exist on when AGI will arrive, no one truly knows when, or even if it's possible. It's tempting to wait until we have robust models for AGI, but the only model we have currently is the human brain. On that basis, it would seem that studying brain functions would lead to faster AGI development. Given how little we really know, a different, more iterative approach makes sense. Indeed, while machines have proven themselves excellent at chess and languages, AGI needs to emulate a toddler. That means instilling foundational skills which become the basis of additional training.

But, foundational skills with additional training implies that learning is purely cause and effect. Human intelligence that includes emotions, goals and instinct is also largely developed for survival. Without these ingredients, it's hard to imagine AGI will be similar to human intelligence.

For AGI to enter the real world, it requires robotics to develop abilities, knowledge and understanding. Once it has these things, they can be cloned into other machines. Allowing autonomous intelligence to develop in the real world requires serious consideration to both ethics and safety. It's essential to recognise where AGI can be controlled and limited for the benefit of our species. Not to do so could be catastrophic.

ANI vs AGI: The Limits and the Benefits	
ANI – Artificial Narrow Intelligence	**AGI – Artificial General Intelligence**
AI that handles singular, specific or limited tasks.	AI that's yet to exist. Capable of adapting itself to a wide range of tasks according to circumstance.
Examples include image recognition, processing a mortgage application, chatbots.	Key example being it connects with other specialist machines to handle a wide range of cognitive tasks.
Trained how to complete pre-defined tasks by data scientists.	Learns on its own and can apply existing knowledge to future tasks.
Correlates pre-specified questions to existing datasets to complete the task in question.	Consistently passes a range of different Turing tests.
No capacity to think on its own. No sign of consciousness or self-awareness.	A unified intelligence that demonstrates creativity, common sense and emotional intelligence.

Probably the most well-known company pursuing the development of AGI is Deepmind, a division of Alphabet INC. Founded in 2010, Deepmind was acquired by what was then Google in 2014. The technology is widely referred to as Google Deepmind. Since 2015, Google continues to develop its AI technology on a variety of applications. Deepmind is significant because of the pure research focus of the company. The evolution of this research is worth noting as it shows how such technologies might develop:

Year	Achievement	Why It Matters
2014	Deepmind acquired by Google.	Properly funded with access to exponentially larger datasets on which to learn from.
2016	'AlphaGo' beats human Go grandmaster Lee Sedol in a five-game match.	Unlike Chess, Go is believed to have an intuitive element to the gameplay. Human players have since learned new ways of looking at the game by learning from the way AlphaGo played.
2017	AlphaZero achieves superhuman gameplay in Chess, Go and Shogi, and beats other specialised programmes.	Unlike AlphaGo, it was a generalised system that learned to master each of the games in under twenty-four hours.
2018	Develops a neural network which 'imagines' 3D scenes based from 2D models.	The 'Generative Query Network' reduces a need for labels such as 'ball' or 'frog', instead becoming more capable of 'unsupervised learning' requiring less input from human operators.
2019	Develops an algorithm aimed at boosting wind-energy efficiency.	Google reports a 20% energy production increase after installing the AI software across its major renewable energy facilities in the US.
2020	AlphaFold uncovers 98.5% of protein structures of the human proteome.	Prior to AlphaFold, we knew the 3D structures for around 17% of the 20,000 proteins in the human body. This was the first time a serious scientific problem had been solved by AI and opens the floodgates to new research, medicine development and bioengineering.
2022	Deepmind unveils AlphaCode, an AI capable of creating computer programmes at a similar rate to that of a human programmer.	Has the potential to turn complicated programming challenges into working code.

All of Deepmind's current achievements are significant in the field of deep learning. What they're not is generalised intelligence. The research is costly, time-consuming and requires seriously talented people. The ultimate goal is as it's always been – to build an AGI that can solve everything!

Artificial Super Intelligence

Artificial Super Intelligence (ASI) refers to a software-based system with intellectual powers beyond those of humans across a comprehensive range of categories and fields of endeavour. Individual human IQ typically ranges between 70 and 130. Some computer scientists and futurists theorise that ASI could demonstrate an IQ into the multiple tens of thousands, massively transcending human intelligence.

The idea of machines reaching ASI is often referred to as the 'technological singularity'. This term describes the point at which machines are beyond human control and their continued development is irreversible.

ASI would, by definition, be exponentially better than humans at anything. That includes anything scientific, mathematical, sports-related, medicine or even emotional relationships. Its memory would be infinitely better than ours and it would be able to analyse and process situations faster than we ever could.

Without control mechanisms, an ASI would certainly transform human reality in wildly unpredictable ways. In Nick Bostrom's 2014 book, *Superintelligence*, he discusses the issue of control with a story, 'The Unfinished Fable of Sparrows'.

In the story, some sparrows wanted to control an owl as a pet. All the sparrows loved the idea, except for one who was concerned about what would happen if they lost control of the owl. The other sparrows dismissed this concern by explaining that 'they'd deal with the problem when it happens'. Elon Musk is also concerned about ASI and sees humans as the sparrows and ASI as the owl. Bostrom and Musk are rightly concerned about controlling ASI, as there may only be one chance to get it right.

Forecasts on when singularity will arrive are wide-ranging. However, the general consensus among experts is that it will arrive before the end of the twenty-first century. Another point worth considering is that it could arrive very quickly after AGI. That's because AGI not only has the ability to process all available data, it will also tend to build new AIs aimed at superseding itself. This will eventually (and, according to some viewpoints, 'eventually' means a matter of seconds) mean arriving at technological singularity.

The other major foundational technology of the future is the less-talked-about biotechnology.

BIOTECHNOLOGY

Alongside AI, I've no doubt whatsoever that biotechnology is the second technology that will drive progress in the twenty-first century. But, what is it?

Biotechnology is simply technology based on understanding and leveraging biology. It's nothing new: the bread and cheese you enjoy is a result of biological processes humans recognised thousands of years ago. The milk in your fridge stays fresh because of commercial-scale pasteurisation, which started in 1901.

Biotechnology offers solutions to some of the most pressing challenges facing our species. UN forecasts on global population growth estimate population figures reaching 8.5 billion by 2030, 9.7 billion by 2050 and 10.4 billion by 2100. If this is true, one of the greatest challenges facing us will be how to keep all those mouths fed. To do so, we will need to develop crops that are more resistant to pests and diseases, which, in turn, will increase food production and reduce the need for harmful pesticides. But disease will not be the only issue, climate change is already making it more difficult to grow crops in some areas, especially in Sub-Saharan countries and South Africa. Biotech will improve our understanding of the natural world and allow us to develop technologies that can benefit society in the face of such resource scarcity.

Biotech is already being used to study the genetics of diseases and to develop new drugs and medical treatments that improve human health. Again, in a more populous world, this matters, as we will need to reduce the burden of disease on individuals and the wider society. Imagine a day when we can eradicate age-related illness and facilitate more independent living in older generations.

Biotech will also be critical in reducing our dependence on fossil fuels and driving innovation in renewable forms of energy. We already use biotechnology to produce biofuels that are used as alternatives to fossil fuels. Bioengineered yeast and bacteria will be developed to create fuels from plants and waste material, contributing to a sustainable source of energy in the future.

There's also the economic impact. One forecast from Biospace indicates the market size for Biotech rising from $853 billion in 2020 to $3.4 trillion in 2030. Advances in the field will generate new industries and businesses, which will create employment and stimulate economic growth. The resulting innovation and progress will improve the quality of life for people around the world.

Biotech and Covid-19

The Covid-19 pandemic impacted everyone's daily lives and changed our world forever. At the time of writing, we are entering a more manageable, endemic phase of the virus. The biotechnology industry was profoundly important in helping the world understand what Covid-19 was, developing medicines to treat it and, ultimately, developing a suite of vaccines to protect against the worst impacts when we contracted the virus.

The search for solutions to Covid-19 demonstrated the need for collaboration across the biotech industry. 'Companies jumped in because they wanted to help solve the global crisis. It was their challenge to meet, and they did so,' commented Cartier Esham, Chief Scientific Officer at the Biotechnology Innovation Organisation. It was an all-hands-on-deck moment for biotech. Companies quickly shifted their focus away from their day-to-day research projects to find solutions to the challenge of their professional lives. Many saw this work as a moral choice, which led to an openness that is not often seen in pharmaceuticals. Twist Bioscience, for example, created synthetic versions of Covid-19 for other biotech research organisations. Doing so minimised the need for unnecessary exposure to the real virus.

There was significant polarisation among the general public, particularly about the use of new vaccines. However, one survey from Service Research Insights reports that 'the extraordinary effort made to develop safe and effective vaccines, shows that positive ratings of pharmaceutical companies went from 32% in early 2020 to 62% in early 2021'. The pandemic created two positive outcomes for biotechnology. First, the increase in collaboration showed the industry and general public what was possible when science was harnessed at speed and without barriers. Second, it enhanced the public perception of the biotech industry as a whole.

Possibly the best-known evolution of biotechnology is the Human Genome Project. Our DNA contains the instructions that shape our development from embryo to death. Sequencing technology has developed so quickly that whereas mapping an individual human genome in 2001 cost US$100 million, by 2022 the same process cost just US$600. Researchers are building new understanding about diseases, from viruses to cancers. And this is leading to novel medications and more accurate predictions about their effects on individual patients and whole populations.

Cost of mapping the human genome:

2001 = US$ 100m
2022 = US$ 600

DNA sequencing is also foundational to the growing field of **genomics**. Tools like CRISPR allow geneticists to edit parts of the genome just as you would cut and paste text in a document. In 2021, CRISPR was already in clinical trials to treat sickle cell disease, which affects millions of people worldwide. The current treatment is a bone marrow transplant, which is risky and can have severe complications, particularly if the patient's body rejects the foreign cells. CRISPR solves this problem because it treats the patient's own cells. If such biotech innovations prove successful, it will herald more interventions for genetic diseases.

Increasingly, biotech research will combine with other scientific disciplines, including materials science, physics, chemistry and engineering, to manipulate living organisms and their component parts and produce incredibly useful products. Expect to see significant advances in medicine environmental science, energy and food production and military solutions with biotechnology as the foundational layer.

Alongside AI and biotech as the technological building blocks of the future, our lives will be significantly influenced and impacted by a range of core technologies from geoengineering to tech interfaces that will blur our very understanding of reality.

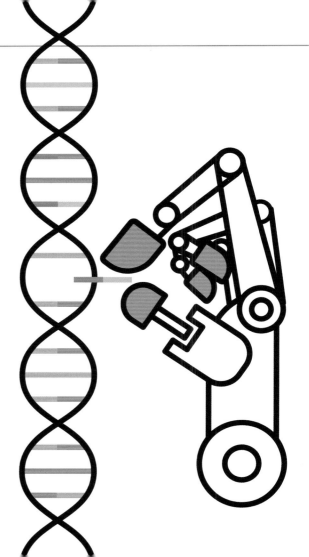

GEOENGINEERING

The threat of climate change isn't going away. A report from the United Nations Environment Programme (UNEP) in October 2022 insists that plans to reach the Paris Agreement's goal of limiting global temperature rise to 1.5°C above pre-industrial levels simply isn't realistic. The report forecasts that even if all participating nations deliver their plans in full by 2030, it'll only represent a 10% fall in emissions, not the 45% reduction required to deliver such a result.

So, perhaps the time has come to address previously taboo technologies that will buy us time to move away from polluting fossil fuels. Some commentators think we need to be discussing the opportunities and dangers associated with geoengineering. Broadly speaking, these technologies either remove carbon from our atmosphere or reflect sunlight away from the planet so less heat is absorbed in the first place. If we're honest, burning massive quantities of fossil fuels since the Industrial Revolution has been an inadvertent (and, in hindsight, horrendous) example of geoengineering. At a smaller scale, countries including the US have used cloud seeding technologies to create snow and rainfall. One notable example was how Beijing's Weather Modification Office sprayed silver iodide into clouds before they reached the Olympic stadium in 2008. The effect being that rainclouds were 'flushed' before they reached the city. In fairness to the initiative, it can't be truly described as geoengineering as the quantities of chemicals were tiny and the effects localised. Projects like these are a long way from modifying the global climate system.

Geoengineering is very controversial. Critics argue that small-scale experiments could reach a tipping point as they increase in size. That tipping point could have all sorts of unintended consequences as geoengineering interacts with naturally occurring processes. It's a collection of technologies that has no national boundaries and introduces complex geopolitical questions. Even if we get the technologies right, can we agree at a global level on whether to deploy them? If we can't, what's to stop a single country (or even an individual) from deploying them? As climate challenges multiply, could the introduction of such technologies spark future conflict or full-scale wars as countries are affected in different ways? Once we start playing God with the climate, it's a Pandora's box situation. When we fix one problem, we could easily start another. And, finally, we wouldn't know the consequences without actually trying it.

There are also dangers in not trying geoengineering. Researchers and scientists all acknowledge it's not the best solution. They're rightly concerned that as society continues to build fossil-fuel power plants, vehicles and cities, these will all continue to create greenhouse gases for decades to come. Therefore, not to explore technology that could mitigate loss of life, species and ecosystems would be negligent at the very least.

So, yes, geoengineering is risky. However, we already see climate-driven famine, fires, extinction and migration, and as these increase, it is not unlikely that policy makers, politicians and the wider public start to ask whether modifying the planet's atmosphere is a risk we can't afford not to take?

So, let's look at what these technologies actually consist of:

Artificial trees:
Researchers at Arizona State University claim to have developed a 'mechanical' tree which absorbs CO2 up to 1,000 times faster than a naturally occurring tree. Once captured, the carbon is sequestered or reused for practical applications.

Enhanced photosynthesis:
Manipulating plants, trees and algae to become more efficient at photosynthesis. The idea being they metabolise more CO2 and store it in the ground.

Cloud seeding:
Sometimes referred to as Marine Cloud Brightening, involves spraying a fine mist of seawater into cloud. The idea being to make cloud reflect more sunlight back into space.

Alkalinity addition:
Our oceans absorb roughly 25% of CO2 emitted in our atmosphere. This contributes to a process called 'ocean acidification'. The theory of increasing alkalinity by dissolving minerals in our oceans is that their capacity to sequester CO2 would increase as a result.

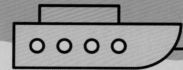

Ocean fertilisation:
Works by dumping iron sulphate or Urea into areas of low biological productivity. The theory is this stimulates phytoplankton growth. The resulting phytoplankton absorb CO2, die, then fall to the seafloor where the carbon is sequestered.

Space mirrors:
Billions of free-floating mirrors take solar radiation and reflect it back to space. A steerable network of mirrors could physically reduce the world's heat, but also have unintended consequences such as drought and warming the poles, thus adding to sea-level increases.

Reflective aerosols:
Proposals include spraying reflective particles such as calcium carbonate, powdered salt or sulphur dioxides into the stratosphere. Like space mirrors, these particles would reflect solar radiation back into space. The risks of droughts increase, and computer simulations estimate it could endanger food and water sources for 2 billion people. Hundreds of civil society organisations are already calling for a multilateral ban on solar engineering in general.

Artificial upwelling:
Artificially moving nutrient-rich deep ocean water to the surface. The result being that new phytoplankton grow, absorb CO_2, die, then fall to the seafloor, where the carbon is sequestered.

Direct injection:
Pressurised CO_2 is injected into geological formations, where it can be stored for extended periods. It's even been used in the UK's North Sea to aid the extraction of natural gas, leaving the CO_2 in place of the gas.

CO2 storage:
CO_2 is captured from power stations or other industrial plants at the point of emission. Typically, it's mixed with a chemical, then pumped underground for long-term storage.

PHYGITAL: THE NEW REALITY

You might ask why 'Phygital' and what do I mean? We're talking about the world of 'spatial computing'. Instead of interacting with static devices through keyboards, including laptops and mobile devices, we'll increasingly interact with machines in physical space. Therefore, it is important to explore what these technologies are, how they work and what they could mean for us moving forward.

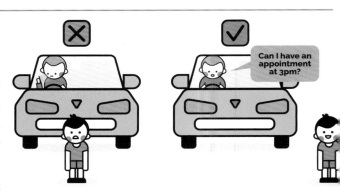

Our mobile devices, ubiquitously **touchscreen**, place the world at our fingertips twenty-four hours a day. It's not just our personal devices, touchscreens are everywhere – busy high streets, airports, industrial estates, etc.

Arguably, it was Apple that mainstreamed the touchscreen interface after purchasing Fingerworks in 2005. It was their iGesture pad – a PDA device that allowed one-handed gesturing – that formed the basis of their touchscreen phones and music players in 2007. We're all familiar with touchscreen, but a growing trend is the use of voice assistants. Research firm Gartner stated that a third of all internet searches were conducted by **voice** in 2020. And Searchengineland writes that 48% of all consumers use voice to find information when they have limited time and need answers quickly. Why? Because it reduces the friction between us and the answers we need.

Voice systems can make us safer drivers. The UK's Transport Research Laboratory showed in a 2020 report that 'driver distraction' levels are much lower when using mapping applications through voice. This matters, as 30% of vehicle collisions across Europe are estimated to be caused by driver distraction. It turns out that voice assistants are also very popular with the elderly. In 2019, Voicebot.ai reported that 20% of the over-sixties owned a smart speaker and nearly half used it daily. Removing the barriers of small touchscreens and keyboards has helped older people live better, more independent lives, even when alone. Voice assistants facilitate basic needs, like enabling food shopping, calling medical assistance and helping young children stay in touch or learn even before they are able to dial a number or work a keypad. A voice assistant could enable a person with a disability to do in five seconds what otherwise might take five minutes through another technology.

Without doubt, voice assistants are already playing a more apparent role in our everyday lives, and it's an interface that we can continue to leverage for productivity, entertainment and general ease of living. However, there's an even more interesting interface on the horizon.

Twenty years ago, you might remember the film *Minority Report*. If you've watched it, you'll remember seeing Tom Cruise interacting with a large transparent screen using a pair of gloves. It's all happening

quickly – he's controlling videos, zooming in and out, and selecting the items he needs. One thing that hit me at the time was the speed with which he interacts with the computer. That's **gesture control**. It recognised his hand gestures perfectly and enabled him to work practically at the same speed as his thoughts.

At the time, that scene seemed like pure science fiction. Not only is it completely achievable today, but we're beyond it. Even a US$299 VR headset from Meta lets users eliminate controllers altogether. Ever since 2018, I've been using a gesture controller to control slides during keynote presentations. The one I use is a gesture-based armband that draws input from muscular contractions and movement.

One of the challenges for advanced gesture recognition has been accurately recognising movement, identifying it, then translating it quickly into commands for applications. Until machine learning emerged into the mainstream, the technology typically needed clear backgrounds and well-lit conditions – that's not the everyday reality of people who just want to get stuff done in the car, at home or in the street.

Another significant challenge is that it requires people to learn a new 'gesture-based' language.

For example, a fist opening to palm could trigger opening an application. An open palm contracting to fist could be the command to close it. Those are singular examples. More sophisticated commands would include combining gestures.

For example, moving fingers clockwise and showing your thumb could be used to mark an area on screen, perhaps highlighting groups of files. There's also a diversity issue – how I wave is different to how you do. That's where machine learning comes into its own, drawing from thousands of similar gestures to aid classification. After all, you'd hate to accidentally delete the family photo album with an inadvertent finger movement!

EgoGesture have already started to create this new language with a dataset for egocentric hand gesture recognition that shows eighty-three classes of static and dynamic gestures focused on interaction with wearable devices. These are just individual – imagine what happens when you start to combine them.

It's still early days for gesture recognition, particularly for mainstream adoption. Gesture recognition systems will need to become intuitive and that means building a common set of gestures that can be controlled by all applications. There will of course be instructions requiring specialist movements. Perhaps it'll be like playing the guitar: easy to learn the basic chords, but a steep learning curve to play like Jimi Hendrix. There's also a privacy aspect to consider. For gesture recognition to go mainstream, we'll need efficient algorithms and hardware to compute what's being communicated. Our gestures are yet another form of data – do we want to give it away to remote server systems? Or worse still, inadvertently give away security information as we gesture control our bank account at the local Starbucks!

Regardless of pitfalls, gesture recognition offers us a range of new opportunities. In consumer electronics, it's totally feasible we'd want to use our hands to interact with home media applications. Playing a film, adjusting the volume, muting sound – all quickly and easily done with embedded cameras. Or in our smart homes – turning lights on and off or dimming them with the flick of a wrist.

In healthcare, gesture recognition could be used to maintain sterile surgical wards – surgeons could quickly review assistive documentation or control a camera without touching a screen (or paper for that matter).

In entertainment, game controllers are currently widely used but Microsoft Kinect has already proven they're not needed. Full body gaming allows for greater immersion, especially in home-fitness applications.

Both voice and gesture control are easy to grasp (forgive the pun), elsewhere the very frontiers of reality are being explored.

Mixed-Reality Devices and the Metaverse

I'd be very surprised if you haven't come across the terms VR, AR or metaverse by now.

AR (augmented reality) and VR (virtual reality) are component technologies of MR (mixed reality). Put simply, AR adds a layer of computer-generated information over the real world, either with a mobile or glasses/lenses. Perhaps your children played Pokemon Go a few years ago; or, you've used a mobile device to translate a paper-based menu while on holiday. Both are current examples of AR in practice. VR is different. It involves wearing a headset to create completely computer-generated environments which typically provide a 360° view.

AR will have a significant impact on a wide range of industries and applications. Just as the mouse did for keyboards, it could revolutionise how we interact with technology and the world around us. It could be used in education to create immersive learning experiences and in entertainment to create new forms of interactive content. Back in 2020, I worked with a major retail operator exploring new revenue opportunities. One idea we discussed was to audit the 'dead air' (unused space) inside their shopping malls. We explored how AR could be introduced outside of the retail units for games, art exhibitions and more. They have since opened a dedicated in-house agency and are developing pilot projects using the technology.

AR will change the way that we work and communicate. It's already used in construction to provide workers with real-time information and instructions. AR models enable remote project managers to check site progress and ensure that plans are being executed correctly. It's also being used in communication to allow people to interact with each other in new and more immersive ways.

Kay Poh Gek Vasey

Founder and Chief Connecting Officer, MeshMinds and The MeshMinds Foundation

As a 'recovering' lawyer, who comes from the world of words, I have developed a deep passion and interest in how we can supercharge storytelling by harnessing the old adage 'a picture speaks a thousand words'.

The earliest forms of human storytelling were oral, with stories being passed from generation to generation. Later, these became visual, in the form of cave paintings. More recently, around 3,400 years ago, were the earliest examples of human writing, which, even then, were pictorial in the form of hieroglyphics.

Digital storytelling is the most rapidly evolving form of storytelling that was first developed with the invention of individual computers in 1948. For me, the rise of augmented and virtual reality, along with advances in the gaming world, are exciting because these technologies are bringing us closer to a gesture-controlled future that is driven by visual literacy.

In 2021, I worked with the UN Environment Programme on a series of augmented reality games that invited people to shake their heads when they saw polluting plastics on their smartphone screens. We focused on linking the real-world gesture that we wanted people to do whilst making a pledge to 'say no' to single-use plastic, moving away from standard mobile games played with thumbs. By gamifying the call to action in this way, we engaged over 1.2 million young people across Southeast Asia to change their habits and created a ripple effect to catalyse long-lasting behaviour change.

Despite the phrase 'augmented reality' being coined in 1990, it's still a technology very much in its infancy. Its impact as a key technology interface layer for the twenty-first century is barely felt right now.

The majority of AR users currently use mobile devices to access the technology. However, that could be set to change. At the time of writing, Apple is very bullish on AR. CEO Tim Cook was even quoted as saying, *'I regard AR as a big idea like the smartphone. The smartphone is for everyone. I think AR is that big. It's huge.'* Even back in 2019, the company had fifty-nine patents granted around the technology. Fast forward to 2023, the technology press is rumouring they are about to release a high-end set of AR glasses.

The next iteration is a move to so-called 'invisible computing'. Companies like Mojo are working on contact lenses that contain advanced hardware, eye-tracking software and communications built in. It provides wearers access to real-time information, while being entirely invisible to anyone looking at them. Its hardware continuously tracks eye movement so that information is available to users wherever their gaze is focused. The applications are endless. Athletes could use the Mojo lens to train smarter and reach their peak performance levels, reacting to real-time data without having to adjust their movement. Ultimately it could be an invisible assistant that people use throughout their day. With well-designed applications, it would certainly help people to access information that aids their confidence in any situation. Although, it is easy to see the sinister side, too, in which people can profile each other without their knowledge.

The parallel to AR is VR and metaverse.

From AR to VR, and Beyond

Virtual reality makes it possible for people to experience things in a truly immersive and interactive way, allowing them to feel fully present in a virtual environment. Applications include gaming, education, training, and more.

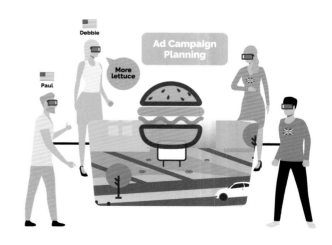

For me, a major application is its capacity to facilitate remote collaboration and meetings that help people to feel as if they are in the same physical space, regardless of where they are in the physical world. In an increasingly hybrid world this could be an incredibly powerful way of transforming the way we work and socialise. Indeed, this blurring of worlds has given rise to the concept of the metaverse.

Science fiction often shows us versions of a possible future. Ernest Cline's novel *Ready Player One* (subsequently turned into a major film) depicts its characters nearly constantly immersed into an alternative computer-generated world. Nowadays, the term 'metaverse' is often applied to describe these alternative realities. Despite its dystopian outlook, there are real positives to draw from the concept.

If you have younger or teenage children, it's quite possible some of their time is spent gaming in virtual worlds already. Examples being Roblox, Minecraft, Fortnite or the now ancient Second Life. Within these worlds, they are able to game out scenarios before committing to a course of action. A great thing about virtual worlds is you can fail at something and start again. People

Haptic suits even enable a sense of touch'

comfortable with failure can keep going until they get the solution right. That can do wonders for a sense of resilience. Exploring and learning in games equals curiosity. Curiosity is a critical character trait in a fast-changing world.

In the physical world, there's a tendency for people to judge first impressions of others based on how they look. When strangers meet in the virtual world, there's a greater likelihood of judgment being based on how they respond to each other and the abilities they bring. The result of which is the way a virtual world facilitates collaboration between people who otherwise might not have met or engaged with

Climate pods enable a sense of weather'

each other. In *Ready Player One*, the characters came together from extremely diverse backgrounds, but there wasn't even a discussion about backgrounds. In this way, the opportunities for creative teams such as designers and engineers to communicate, analyse, decide and execute projects inside metaverse environments is truly inspiring. Contingent teams will come together, create, then disband, moving onto the next project.

What does this tell us? Well, in their virtual worlds the next generation are learning the skills that will enable their positive futures. Operating in machine-generated environments, learning to collaborate with other people while exploiting the technology is giving them an edge that those who aren't won't have. It's foolhardy to

Even real world smells can be generated'

forecast when the metaverse will become mainstream, but it's obvious that employers must embrace this new breed of digital natives if they want to thrive in the future economy.

Ultrasonic actuators create a sense of touch.

If the metaverse feels too sci-fi for you, then the next tech interface is straight from *Star Trek*'s 'Holodeck'.

Trekkies may remember that this deck created a 3D simulation of a real or imaginary setting in which the crew could interact with the environment, objects and characters. Well, 3D holograms are on the cusp of entering our lives. A 3D hologram is an object that isn't actually 'there', but looks like it is. It could be floating in mid-air or standing on a surface. Both Samsung and LG have been working on holographic displays for over a decade. It's a technology in its infancy, but one to watch for. I'm mentioning it, as gesture control will be the way we interact with these environments when they do mainstream. Air-swiping is just the beginning; through infinity floors we'll interact with holographic environments in exactly the way we do in real life – combining gestures with voice.

In fact, it's all too possible that we'll quickly overleap the need to explicitly communicate with tech at all and our brains will do it all for us through direct brain-machine connections or neural interfaces.

Neural Interfaces

Brain Machine Interfaces (BMIs) are nothing new. Indeed, German psychiatrist Hans Berger invented the electroencephalography (EEG) in 1924. EEGs are a way of measuring electrical activity in the brain, which are often referred to as brainwaves. The EEG is widely used today in diagnosing medical conditions and psychological practices. Outside of medicine, EEGs are even used in market research, looking at the 'P300' signal, which measures intent. That could include monitoring buying decisions or voting choices. Neural Interfaces differ from BMIs in that they facilitate a connec-

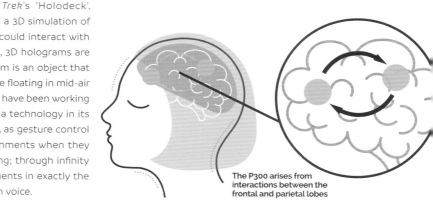

The P300 arises from interactions between the frontal and parietal lobes

tion with the peripheral nervous system and spine. For example, this could enable advanced prosthetic limbs. Essentially, there are two types of neural interfaces:

Dry

1. The 'dry' interface that indirectly and specifically measures brain activity.

2. The 'wet' interface that involves chips or electrodes being inserted directly into the brain or spinal cord.

Wet

The principal idea behind full neural interfaces is that there will be a read/write capacity. That is to say, machines could understand us, and even write information directly to our brains. It's also theorised that a form of telepathy would be possible between humans. That's probably a way off, as the most we can reliably do right now is interpret the motor neurons that control a prosthetic limb.

That said, there are experiments taking place. In 2019, researchers from the University of Washington conducted one that involved three people playing Tetris by measuring electrical activity from their brains. Five groups of three participants were asked to 'connect' to play sixteen rounds of the game; thirteen of the sixteen rounds resulted in success in which the blocks were rotated and cleared. That's an 81% success rate. The researchers used the experiment to pave the way for future brain-to-brain interfaces aimed at solving complex problems. They also began co-operating with the

neuroethics team at the Center for Neurotechnology to address privacy concerns, especially as the technology becomes more sophisticated. They weren't the first, either. Kaspersky, the computer antivirus company, even forecast a new industry 'antivirus for the human body'. For example, it could one day be desirable to hack a user's P300 signal to influence advertising and even buying choices. Those would be pretty mundane exploitations compared to say, forcing a user to commit a crime against their will or committing crime against another user. Any networked device with an IP address can be hacked. Pacemakers can already be instructed to deliver a lethal pulse, thus potentially kill the user. In the future, our neural interfaces could be triggered to have us commit our own murder/suicide.

'The bad news is when your heart is an IP address, then it's also subjected to denial of service attacks, malware, and other types of problems. By the way, that punk kid, 17 year old, in his mom's basement next door, now has access to your heart too,' Mark Goodman, Futurist

Certainly, the science is beginning to catch up with the science fiction. 'Neurotech' companies are starting to capitalise on scientific developments with tangible products that solve real-world problems. However, current developments are in the very early stages of this technology. When the Wright brothers first flew a heavier-than-air plane in 1903, it'd be fair for humans to say 'we can fly', but they wouldn't have dreamed of international jetliners or a rocket to the moon coming just a few decades later. Think of neurotech right now as 'we can fly'.

Brain-computer interfaces broadly fall into two categories. The first being medical and restorative:

ENHANCING AND AUGMENTATION

MEDICAL AND RESTORATIVE

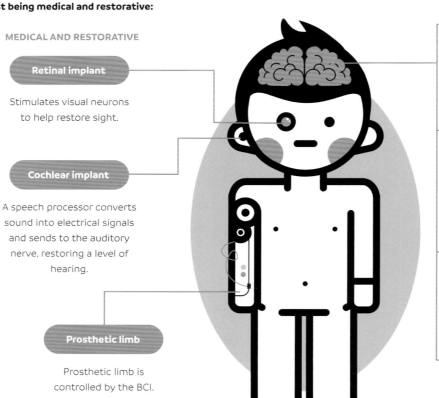

Retinal implant

Stimulates visual neurons to help restore sight.

Cochlear implant

A speech processor converts sound into electrical signals and sends to the auditory nerve, restoring a level of hearing.

Prosthetic limb

Prosthetic limb is controlled by the BCI.

Neurotutoring

A BCI application that analyses brain activity, then tailors learning to the mental state of the learner in real-time.

Enhanced computer games

A BCI application that adapts the game experience in response to the player's thoughts, emotions and desired outcomes in real time.

Mind-reading

Translating inner speech to communication, either with computers or other human beings.

Robot assistant

Controlling a physical machine or robot using the power of thought alone.

This technology throws up a range of very serious issues:

OUR PRIVACY	» Who gets access to the data created by us as we use the technology? » Can we ever know our inner most thoughts are truly ours? » Will our voting choices, buying decisions, etc. be tracked (and even influenced) without our knowledge?
HUMAN EQUALITY	» If only the wealthy can afford augmentative BMIs, such as brain enhancement, do the rest of us become second-class citizens? » Will governments be ready and equipped to handle neuroethics and prevent misuse of the technology? » What about governments in the Global South – will they be left behind?
PERSONAL RESPONSIBILITY (MORAL AND CONTROL ISSUES)	» If a remotely controlled robot damages property or hurts another human being, where does responsibility lie – with the operator or the robot? » If the robot detects an unconscious human thought then acts on it, who is responsible for the action?
SAFETY AND SECURITY	» Physical safety: if we have a direct implant in our body, what are the risks of malfunction? » Hacking: what are the risks of unauthorised access? Will antivirus for the human body be sufficient protection? » Undesired influence: could BMIs amplify the risk of epilepsy? Or affect our memory capacity negatively? » Dependence: as calculators reduced our dependence on arithmetic, could BMIs create new forms of dependence such as reliance on external processing for simple decision making?
LOSS OF HUMANITY	» As we become more enmeshed with machines, where is the line between humanity and machines? When do human rights become machine rights and vice versa? » If a machine can alter our thought processes, where does human identity stop and start? » Does religion play a part? Believers in deities may question the right of machines to interfere in human nature.

The table on the previous page paints a pretty bleak picture of neural interfaces; however, it is possible to see more practical and positive realities. For example, imagine someone walking through their smart city, considering how best to complete the last mile of their commute. Suddenly they see a holographic advert for an e-bike service and in the span of the thought, their neural interface has already subscribed them to the service and arranged for the bike to be picked up the next day.

Subscribe to eBike and get 50 Ziptax credits

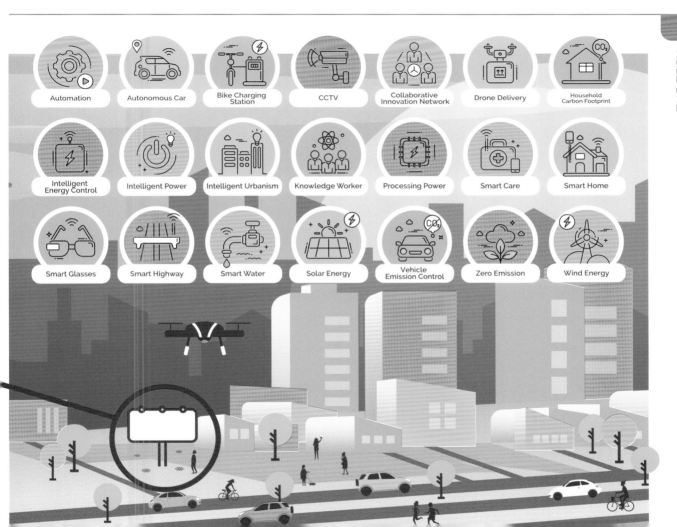

Automation

Autonomous Car

Bike Charging Station

CCTV

Collaborative Innovation Network

Drone Delivery

Household Carbon Footprint

Intelligent Energy Control

Intelligent Power

Intelligent Urbanism

Knowledge Worker

Processing Power

Smart Care

Smart Home

Smart Glasses

Smart Highway

Smart Water

Solar Energy

Vehicle Emission Control

Zero Emission

Wind Energy

TECH YOU MIGHT NOT HAVE THOUGHT OF

So far we've focused on the 'big tech' innovations, but smaller scale, wacky yet wonderful technologies from around the world are coming on stream that have the potential to make our lives better. It's not all super serious and some of them are pretty conceptual!

WHAT	WHY IT'S NEEDED	WHAT HAPPENS
WARNING LIGHTS FOR SMARTPHONE USERS	People walking in the street cause accidents by looking at their phones instead of where they're going.	Warning lights placed at pedestrian crossings alert people they're about to cross a road.
SWEAT-POWERED ELECTRICITY	Why not?	Sweat interacts with a sensor worn on a fingertip to generate electricity. This even works while the user is asleep. Demonstrates the concept of effortless wearable power generation.
HIPSAFE FALL PROTECTION AIRBAGS FOR THE ELDERLY	As older people become more frail, falls and tumbles have more serious consequences.	A wearable airbag inflates when the sensor detects a fall. Protective air cushions soften the impact of the fall, which could prevent injuries and save lives.

WHAT	WHY IT'S NEEDED	WHAT HAPPENS
LANDMINE REMOVAL DRONES	By some estimates, there are 110,000,000 landmines in 65 countries left over from previous conflicts. They cause an esti-mated 6,000 injuries and deaths each year.	Mine Kafon builds drone mine detection and removal technology that clears mined areas while keeping costs down and people safe.
GLOW-IN-THE-DARK FOOTPATHS	Reduces the need for artificial lighting. A simple and ingenious safety idea for pedestrians.	Paths include UV absorbing materials that absorb sunlight during the day then glow at night. Easy, simple safety using materials science.
AUGMENTED REALITY GLASSES	AR glasses that help visually impaired people to see better.	AR glasses can project aspects of the world to appear larger than they are, and to appear either in the periphery or central part of the projection, according to the wearer's eye weakness/strength/needs. They will also allow wearers to, for example, zoom in to hard-to-see things like small text.
LEKA – A TOY FOR NEURODIVERGENT CHILDREN	Designed to support neurodivergent chil-dren with their emotional responses and interactions in social situations.	Leka uses interactive play to learn life skills and gain greater autonomy. It adapts itself to the child's specific needs as well.

THE TECH – HACKER HINTS

The following questions serve as hints for concepts you might want to ponder further to get future-ready.

Human-technology progress will be a co-evolution

Questions to ask yourself:

- » Are you clear on the changes that technology will bring to your life?
- » What impacts do you think AI will have on your workplace? Are you ready for them?
- » Are you open to change and ready to adjust yourself for it?
- » How will you go about reskilling or changing career, if needed?
- » Are you willing to explore the new breed of AI tools?

Dealing with climate change will require bold choices

Questions to ask yourself:

- » How do you feel about geoengineering as a means of handling the climate crisis?
- » What actions could you personally take to address climate change issues?
- » Are you curious about 'climate smart' products?
- » Can you change your consumption patterns to use more 'climate smart' products?

Interacting with sophisticated technology is getting easier

Questions to ask yourself:

- » Do you feel that you may have lost agency with the world as a result of using technology?
- » What are the consequences of this? Do the gains perhaps outweigh that lost sense of agency?
- » What new forms of agency have you acquired through the use of sophisticated technology?

THE WORKPLACE

THE WORKPLACE

I frequently use the expression 'Jobs are only going away when problems go away' in keynote speeches about the future of work. It's a very succinct way of helping audiences understand the fabric of jobs, businesses and other organisations. In short, new jobs emerge because society has new problems that need solving. Older jobs phase out because those problems either don't exist or have been solved by other means.

Let's look at a few jobs that simply don't exist anymore. Some will seem bizarre, almost silly, but each shows us how far society has evolved:

Job Title	What it involved
Knocker-Upper	Knocker-Uppers were a common sight on the streets of Britain, pre-1950s. That's because we didn't have reliable alarm clocks, so we needed a human with a long stick to walk the streets and tap on workers' windows.
Ice Cutter	Before mechanical refrigeration arrived in 1930s, making ice was a dangerous affair. It involved workers bringing equipment and horses to frozen lakes, then cutting out chunks of ice. Frostbite was common and the risk of falling through the ice ever-present.
Linkboy	Before streetlights were common in seventeenth-century London, young boys would be hired at night to light torches and guide patrons from taverns to home or other places.
Scribe	Before printing was invented, scribes would copy manuscripts by hand, word for word. By the fourteenth century, early mass printing arrived, rendering the scribe redundant
Pinsetter	In the early 1900s, young men were hired by bowling alleys to reset pins after they had been knocked over by bowling balls. By the early 1950s, the automatic pinsetter arrived, rendering the human being unemployed.

**Conversely, let's look at a few examples of jobs that should evolve
to answer future problems:**

Job Title	What it will inolve
Water Harvester	With climate change will come higher temperatures. In some regions, that could be lethal. As water evaporates from one area, it may fall as rainwater in another. Step forward, the 'Water Harvester'. This person installs sophisticated technology to extract the moisture from air in order to provide drinking water where it's needed.
Metaverse Concierge	If 3D worlds evolve as spaces to live and work, busy people will continue to value their time. It will be a premium service, which could involve acting as a guide to the metaverse itself or assisting with specific tasks like online shopping. Obviously, machines will do a lot of this, but there will be a premium for the human touch.
Ageing Specialist	Better healthcare and investments into the human longevity movement mean people are living longer than ever. In 1990, just 95,000 people lived to 100 globally. The World Economic Forum forecasts that could rise to 3.7 million by 2050. To help people live independently and for longer, we'll need consultants to show older people how to best use a growing range of technologies to help them do just that.
Intergenerational Leadership Coach	There are now three to four generations of people in the current workforce. As people live longer, that number could rise as high as five or six. Managers will need coaching on the similarities and differences between each generation to maximise productivity and remain fully effective.
Digital Addiction Therapist	If you thought smartphone addiction was a thing, you haven't seen anything yet. Imagine AI-fuelled virtual reality experiences that adjust themselves on-the-fly in response to facial expressions, pupil dilation, perspiration and heartrate. The depression and anxiety resulting from a return to the 'real world' by some will need treatment and care by skilled professionals.

If you want to understand where jobs of the future will come from, it's worth spending time considering what the future problems for society will be. You may already be able to spot this for yourself. For example, a friend of mine was a successful barrister. She was always interested in technology and space travel. As she explored her interests further, she realised that commercial space exploration and exploitation was only increasing. There was even talk of 'Asteroid Mining' for rare earths and precious metals. What did it all mean? A new area of legal precedent would emerge to create the ground rules and solve disputes. She's now a successful Space Lawyer working at the cutting edge of a new industry.

This is a classic example of the intersection between human skills and technological change that will characterise the evolution of the workplace in the future.

Dr Freija Duijne
Strategic Foresight Practitioner
www.futuremotions.nl

Dashboard Jobs

Back in the day, executive work used to be centered around practical skills. Think, for instance, about the technical skills to operate a machine or harvest a crop. Nowadays, many of these practical jobs are done by machines. Intelligent machines that perform for many hours and are far more consistent than

humans. Does that mean that the people who used to do that work are now out of a job? And that more jobs will be lost in the future due to digitalization and robotization? Generally not. Another type of job is coming up and that requires a different skill set, which is important to be employed in the future.

These digital and robotized systems are being operated through a dashboard display that indicates the state of the system and the parameters to control an optimized workflow. Operators need to manage the system by means of this dashboard. That means they need to oversee the bigger picture of, for instance, the supply chain. They need to communicate more with the other actors in their organization, or their customers.

The necessary work skills are called twenty-first-century skills, which include problem solving, strategic reasoning, communication and compassion. This is far more than the operational skills that were sufficient for the previous generations. Another interesting feature of these so-called dashboard jobs, is that the type of work in different sectors is quite similar. That means people can more easily change from one industry to another.

Those who possess these twenty-first-century skills don't have to fear losing their jobs. There will be plenty of employers who really need them to operate their digitalized production systems.

WILL ROBOTS RULE?

However far AI develops in our lifetimes, it will certainly affect the workplace. When James Watt learned to extract energy from coal, leading to the Steam Engine, it began the Industrial Revolution. This drew people away from agriculture and towards entirely new jobs in urban centres – the modern economy simply wouldn't exist without it. AI will be just as disruptive for us. Entrepreneurs, businesses and other organisations will continue to develop and use this foundational technology to bring about transformation and competitive advantage. Repetitive, process-driven and systematic tasks will be the first to go, such as:

» **Bookkeeping Clerks:** Increasingly being automated by software. Much of this software is already less costly than the equivalent person's salary for the same results.

» **Taxi and Bus Drivers:** There are still very difficult challenges ahead, but forecasts indicate that 1 in 10 vehicles will be self-driving by 2030.

» **Doctors:** Expect to see more robot surgeons performing critical operations because in some cases, such as endoscopic procedures, their work has already been proven to be more effective and less error prone than their human counterparts. This is particularly true where surgical work requires highly repetitive motion and precision.

Moving towards 2030, there are, of course, jobs that can't easily be automated. That's because they require unique human skills to undertake (for now).

» **Chief Executives:** Managing organisations is far from simple. Working with employees is a key CEO's task. Leaders need to motivate teams, resolve conflicts, mentor and more. It requires a range of skills and there's no simple way to teach those skills to a machine. That said, we are already seeing what has come to be called 'Algorithmic Management', whereby, for example, delivery drivers are managed by apps.

» **Editors:** While proofreading software has impacted the editor's work, humans are still needed to check on accuracy, originality and clarity of content. A good editor can infer new patterns and make fresh recommendations to improve the quality of output, whereas software can only correct, not improve.

» **Sales Managers:** Motivating a team to meet targets requires emotional intelligence alongside customer collaboration. They also need to interpret trends, keep an eye on competitor activities and adapt to the markets in which they operate. It's a multi-faceted role, not easily automated due to the innately human aspects of the work.

» **Psychiatrists:** Understanding the human mind is hard. Added to which, humans can express feelings, demonstrate empathy and connect with other people. That's not to say robots won't augment their human counterparts eventually. However, until we reach AGI, human psychiatrists are safe.

From these examples, it seems pretty clear that in the immediate future, AI will take on some jobs, while others are innately human. Robots are less good at humanity (engaging with the rest of us), originality (coming up with things rather than copying them) and complexity (handling the non-numeric, experiential judgements we manage to do without breaking a sweat).

Nevertheless, the dystopian view suggests that the economic inequality gap will widen as millions of hard-working people are automated out of work and unable to make a living. The utopian view is that AI will take over much of the tedium associated with jobs, and governments will step in with a form of 'Universal Basic Income', where every citizen's basic financial needs are taken care of, freeing them up to do other, more fulfilling, creative work. Still, whichever way we look at it, we're going to need to tool ourselves up to work alongside our new non-human colleagues!

SKILLING-UP: 2030 STYLE

The AI-augmented workforce will need new technical skills and massive upskilling. Ultimately, we will have to differentiate and justify our employment by 'becoming more human'.

For example, Google can scrape the internet to give you 1,000 recipes for a meringue. That's a repetitive process which would take humans a long time. But Google couldn't invent a meringue. Invention is a uniquely human creative endeavour (for now).

Creation is just one part of what 'becoming more human' means. We will need a variety of key human skills to propel us forward and thrive in a digitally augmented world, some we can be taught, others we can absorb or glean from the world around us. However we acquire them, these core skills are going to be vital in ensuring that we aren't automated out of the workplace.

The Growing Human Skills Towards 2030

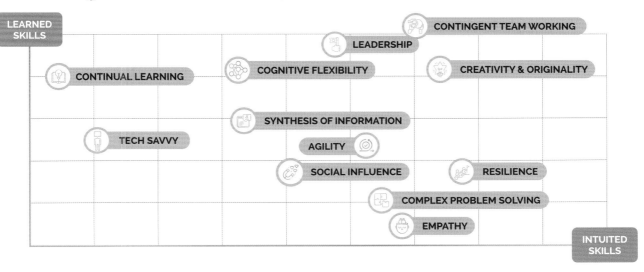

Continual Learning

The McKinsey Global Institute forecasts that 30% of work done globally could be automated by 2030. That same forecast indicates 800 million people globally could lose their jobs. It's not all bleak though. Thriving with increasingly sophisticated AI is about learning skills to augment it; this is why continual learning is so crucial to the future-ready worker and workplace.

Your grandparents may have enjoyed 'a job for life', using skills they learned in their youth that carried them through until retirement.

Not anymore. The increasing speed of technological change means that companies need different skills every five years or so – nobody should think that the skills they learned at school will be enough to last a whole career. Indeed, many companies are worrying that their employees today won't have adequate skills in a matter of just a few years. For example, marketing companies are now aware that it's not enough for their employees to be able to promote a product, they have to be able to master data analytics and behavioural psychology, too.

The skills gap is particularly apparent in two groups of people:

1. **Younger people making their first career steps:** what gets taught in school or university might not connect with what organisations actually need.

2. **Existing workers with many years' experience:** the skills gap can only widen if workers aren't actively learning new skills and technologies.

While AI is an important factor driving the need for continual learning, it's not the only one. There is a confluence of trends:

1. **Human longevity**
   In 2019, life expectancy at birth was 81 years on average across OECD countries – over ten years higher than it was in 1970. And the World Economic Forum suggests the population living to 100 and older is predicted to grow to nearly 3.7 million by 2050, from just 95,000 in 1990. People are living longer and that directly impacts the emerging reality of our working lives.

2. **Technological change**
   The connecting link between increased life expectancy and technological change is that we'll work longer. To do so will require adaptability. To be adaptable, we'll need to maintain our learning as a default position. If we don't, the majority of us will risk losing our employability. It's not all on us as individuals though. Organisations can't protect jobs made redundant by technology – but they do have a responsibility to their people. **Protect people not jobs.** That means future-ready organisations must nurture agility, adaptability and re-skilling. HR and Learning & Development (L&D) teams have a duty to make consistent learning available to all. Failure to do so will only mean talented employees gravitate towards organisations that make continual learning central to their employee strategies.

Firms providing options for continual learning will not only build the skills they need from the inside, but also increase their attractiveness to talent. Interestingly, according to a 2022 ManPower article, four out of five millennials say that learning opportunities are key when selecting a new job or workplace. Quick wins include using Netflix-style systems which provide variety and flexibility at reasonable cost, giving the workforce an eat-as-much-as-you-want buffet of learning. From MOOCs and free short courses run by Yale and Harvard to Coursera and School of Life, there are a host of platforms that enable a life-lessons approach to skilling up. Governments are also endorsing the need for lifelong learners; in the UK a lifelong learning entitlement loan scheme to support people in their search for further knowledge. Of course, there is also a host of information to be found through YouTube, TED talks and the plethora of podcasts now out there for everyone to tap into. Any or all of these will boost your confidence, spark fresh insight, change your perspective and boost your profile. There are some other direct actions you can take:

1. **Organise some storytelling**

   Not all workplace learning needs to be structured and formal. Learning that's laborious doesn't encourage fresh thinking, anyway. You'd be surprised how much latent insight, experience and value colleagues have that they don't share in the workplace. How about, one lunchtime a week, a team member does a presentation on something they enjoy – it could be on cookery, hiking or even a TV series. Not only will it raise awareness about colleagues amongst the wider team, but we learn most when being told stories. It opens us up to thinking differently, which is the very essence of learning itself.

2. **Co-create a learning programme**

   Meaningful learning programmes should be co-created. Too much L&D is foisted onto employees by leaders with an agenda. It doesn't stimulate engagement and it won't reduce the critical skills gap. Establish a team meeting and agree a calendar of events and workshops that centres around themes that your team explicitly want to learn about. It needn't include expensive external consultants and speakers – it could be as simple as watching a ten-minute YouTube clip together and discussing its implications and opportunities for the organisation. By formulating a calendar, it also creates something for the team to look forward to. If you're a leader reading this, don't push your team down specific learning paths. Give them the autonomy to learn what they like. A course on raising alpacas is just fine! Creativity – a key skill for tomorrow's workplaces – arises more naturally when we experience new things in life. Do make part of the learning and development calendar include individuals summarising what they learned to the wider team.

3. **External culture trips**

   Just getting out of the home/office to try new things is a great way to break bad habits that hinder learning and foster learning. Think about breaking through the usual team-building days. It could involve the team visiting a client of a product/service you sell (after all, many employees don't ever meet end customers). Doing so connects the team back to the company's purpose. It can also be a fun experience. I once advised a client to take their team to a virtual reality arcade to try a multi-person game together. Not only did they love the experience, but it gave them new ideas about how they might use VR in their own business. A win-win for sure!

4. **Invite external specialists**

   As an independent futurist, I would say that, wouldn't I? But hear me out. If your organisation is too inward facing, it won't innovate or grow. Bring in specialists periodically to give talks and run short workshops. It boosts knowledge and improves confidence in areas the team may feel weak on, but don't disclose what those are. A great thing about external specialists is their neutrality. They are instantly perceived as independent and are therefore trusted, as their thinking doesn't come from the pre-existing relationships and prejudices of an internal leader.

5. **Use free and low-cost resources**

   If you're part of a small business or start-up, learning and development budgets may be practically non-existent. Don't worry, there's plenty of low-cost and free structured online learning available. Take a look at LinkedIn Learning, FutureLearn, Udemy and even the Open University. These cover the gamut of hard and soft skills that future-ready teams will need.

Tech Savvy

As we've already explored, there's no doubt that **Artificial Intelligence** is becoming the foundational technology layer powering the twenty-first century. For a simple example, we'll come to rely on Virtual Personal Assistants (VPAs) to prepare our online meetings and agendas in advance – a good use of computers removing an annoying task, namely finding a space in people's diaries, fixing an arrangement and communicating it effectively. The tasks that AI will take off our hands will get increasingly complicated, and it will impact virtually every sector and human being in the world.

It will also impact (and accelerate the value of) a range of other emerging technologies; for example, the Internet of Things and Robotics:

» **Internet of Things (IoT)** will continue to find new applications. Abundant and cheap sensors found in smartphone technology will power a range of new applications. Two technologies to watch for include augmented reality smart glasses (Eyewear IoT) and smart clothing. Smart glasses (you may remember the embryonic Google Glass) will layer computer-generated information over real-world environments. Applications for these are wide ranging and include manufacturing and advanced opportunities for colleague collaboration, particularly for remote workers.

IoT enabled smart clothing comes with embedded chips and transmits information about the wearer. Applications include real-time monitoring of worker health and safety in dangerous work environments. Research firm Gartner forecasts that 10% of people will be wearing some form of smart clothing by 2024. If you're wearing a smart watch, you're already ahead of the game.

It's also likely that IoT offices will begin to leverage employee data to assemble teams by algorithmic-driven platforms, with AI creating new internal talent marketplaces in which data on skills and competencies will match people to projects to drive better business outcomes

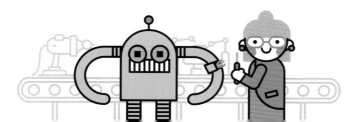

» **Robotics** will become more sophisticated. Expect to see more multipurpose robotics that can easily be used for multiple tasks. Advances in artificial intelligence, machine vision, sensors, motors, hydraulics and materials will change the way products and services are delivered. A surge in tech talent for building, operating and maintaining advanced robots will occur.

To work with these advancing technologies will require tech savvy – a form of digital dexterity. And, according to Gartner, only 9% of current employees have this skill. Ultimately, tech savvy means a willingness and ability to learn new technical skills alongside having an agile mindset that allows you to respond to data quickly and strategically to leverage the best out of the people and resources around you.

Cognitive Flexibility

Cognitive flexibility is our ability to stop one task and quickly move to another. At a higher level, it's an ability to think about multiple ideas/concepts simultaneously. There's even a hybrid sport associated with it called 'Chess Boxing', in which the participants play a round of blitz chess and then a round of boxing until one wins by checkmate or knockout.

Indeed, some may feel that their average workday is not that dissimilar to chess boxing. You certainly need cognitive flexibility to cope with the realities of the twenty-first-century workplace, with its constant change and complexity. For example, consider if automation renders one of your major skills redundant. Or, a more day-to-day example, you're asked to drop what you're doing and join a cross-functional team to solve a serious problem. In a flexible workplace, these are the sorts of things that will happen all the time. Reinventing ourselves professionally will be critical in the future of work.

Synthesis of Information

Leaders are well accustomed to data: management reports are the bread-and-butter of decision making. They analyse it rigorously and decide what to do: it's what the market expects. People can confound the data, too. In 2016, when Donald Trump won the 2016 US election, not a single mainstream opinion poll had predicted his win.

In a changing world, while data offers ever more predictive opportunities, it also offers more opportunities to take us down the wrong path. But we have a tendency to rely on it because it is clear and quantitative. That's even truer for leaders – you can't be criticised for following the numbers.

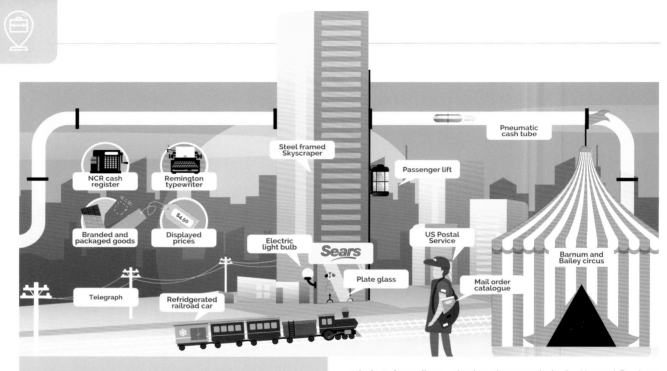

NCR cash register · Remington typewriter · Steel framed Skyscraper · Passenger lift · Pneumatic cash tube · Branded and packaged goods · Displayed prices · $4.50 · Electric light bulb · Sears · US Postal Service · Barnum and Bailey circus · Plate glass · Mail order catalogue · Telegraph · Refridgerated railroad car

An example of a synthesised approach in action is when the US department store Sears revolutionised retail in the nineteenth century by combining a wide variety of innovation of the times to make themselves the go-to physical and mail-order shopping experience.

mindset. According to the American psychologist Howard Gardner: *'The synthsising mind takes information from disparate sources, understands and evaluates that information objectively, and puts it together in ways that make sense to the synthesiser and also to other persons.'*

A synthesising mindset helps you combine multiple data sources and ideas to find new meaning and see the bigger picture in life and work, which is essential in order to build the augmented teams of tomorrow.

Increasingly, AI will handle more analytical tasks on our behalf. We humans had better not try competing with them on this: spotting trends and sifting the fragments of gold from the endless sand of numbers is exactly what computers do best. The way for humans to thrive alongside them is by developing a synthesising

Social Influence

Influencing people is about affecting behaviours in a specific direction, using tactics that involve, connect and inspire people (rather than barking orders). Social influence will matter more than ever because technological change will mean more frequent upheaval, which employees find hard. New business models will require managers at all levels to galvanise support behind a new vision across multiple generations in a workplace where the unquestioning hierarchies of the late twentieth century are gone.

The Centre for Creative Leadership identifies four key skills in leaders which allow them to influence others in an organisation:

» **Organisational intelligence:** People with organisational intelligence understand how to get things done. They embrace the positive (collaboration) and negative (politics) aspects of working in organisations to move teams and important initiatives forward.

» **Team promotion:** Leaders cut through the noise to authentically and credibly promote themselves – while also promoting what's good for the entire organisation.

» **Trust-building:** Because leadership often involves guiding people through risk and change, trust is essential.

» **Leveraging networks:** No leader is an island. They are empowered by their connections with others.

In our fast-changing world, part of effective social influence will be choosing the right tool for the right audience.

For example, older generations might prefer in-person coffee meetings, while the younger groups may have fully embraced Web 3.0 and its associated metaverse technologies by then. If that's the case, get ready to strap on your VR goggles. And even that may not be enough. Generation A (born between 2010–24) 'will need to be engaged differently and they won't understand the hierarchical approach to leadership as they will be used to their voices being heard in a different way through social media', according to Justin Rix of Grant Thornton. The point being that it is not your communication options as a leader that are different; your entire concept of leadership will have to change.

Leadership

'It's really important leaders don't ignore this AI- and data-driven revolution, what I call the 'intelligence revolution' – or allow other leaders in the organization to ignore it.'
Bernard Marr, Futurist.

FUTURE HACKERS

Leaders will need to understand how to use AI tools, handle the associated people-related challenges and be mindful of the ethical and practical pitfalls when choosing/using the right technology for the job. The key aspects of future leadership will be:

» **Technology:** As we've already explored, a multitude of technologies from AI to AR/VR and IoT are going to impact the new workplace. Any leader will need to understand how this tech intersects with the skills of the team and the needs of the organisation.

» **People power:** Forward-thinking organisations will increasingly recognise the value of diversity in the workforce. That's not without its challenges. Generation A will join the working world at this key juncture. In their eyes, purpose will be on-par with or exceed salary as a motivation. Older generations will be accustomed to more hierarchical management structures. The contradictions between generations will require flexible work cultures. Indeed, you can expect a new class of job to emerge: 'Intergenerational Leadership Coaches', who will exist to show leaders the similarities and differences across a widening range of generations, and find ways to keep teams motivated, aligned and sensitive to each other's cultural needs.

» **Developing new skillsets:** Fuelled by rapid technological change, leaders will need to inspire innovation, be adaptive to change and proactively encourage collaboration. Without these key qualities, organisations simply won't remain competitive or fit for purpose. Remember the story of Kodak failing to develop its own innovation – the CCD chipset – which is core to digital cameras? Ultimately it brought the company down because a closed-minded management believed it would cannibalise their existing business. Instead, being vulnerable, celebrating curiosity and experimentation will become business as usual!

» **Articulating and achieving a new vision:** Leaders in the next decade must be willing to break down barriers that slow transformation. This will of course require a clear vision of where the organisation is heading, but it will also demand exceptional communication skills. More honest and direct conversations will be needed to influence teams to support the vision. Only with trust and enthusiastic support can leaders expect employees to implement a vision with the required haste to remain competitive.

» **Learning to think differently:** '*Judgement is easy, thinking is hard.*' This is a quote I often cite when I hear lazy assumptions in the workplace. And thinking is hard! If you're like me, you probably enjoy the less demanding aspects of your work. For example, I love stuffing envelopes. It's borderline meditative. But the big results come from the big changes. Helping teams to adapt, engage and evolve will invariably get messy. Training staff to work with increasingly sophisticated technologies that will augment their work at best and replace it at worst will be simultaneously exciting and threatening. Leaders will need to help their teams negotiate these different ways of thinking to ensure a successful transition.

Agility

For the purpose of discussing 'agility', it's important to define what I mean. It's simply 'our capacity to adapt our mindset in order to think differently about a challenge'.

Agility was something many of us discovered as Covid-19 lockdowns forced new ways of working and learning. Where being present in a physical location had been the norm, organisations, schools and the people in them were forced to adapt quickly to more home-bound ways of living.

Covid-19 was not just a catalyst for change. It was a catalyst for the way change happens. Before it, some organisations would wait for perfect alignment before undertaking significant transformation. The pandemic showed us that life sometimes takes over and forces us to accept rapid change. And it showed us that often (although by no means always), that change works out just fine.

Our need for agility will increase in relation to the frequency of short- and mid-term impacts. Climate change is already increasing the size and frequency of extreme weather events. There's no doubt this will impact supply chains and our ability to deliver goods and services. The increase in our use of smart devices alongside the emergence of AI-enabled hacking software will increase the chances of high-impact cybersecurity attacks. Imagine the consequences of your IT services at work being held hostage by hackers, or an electricity grid being shut down.

A few hints and tips for your own agility:

- » Be ready to respond quickly to new information and insights.
- » Seek out unorthodox views, see both sides and don't be afraid of disagreements or contrary views.
- » Where possible, co-own a problem with partners, stakeholders and customers. Collaborate to find the solution. You don't have all the answers!
- » Build effective feedback loops and make information available quickly, so that teams can communicate effectively. Leaders at the top can only add limited value when developing effective solutions to fast-evolving problems.

On a personal note, the early days of the first lockdown created significant uncertainty for both me as a futurist, but also my wider ModComms business. Before Covid-19 struck, ModComms had a side venture running a pop-up virtual reality arcade to support corporate events. Demand disappeared overnight during lockdown. We invested in more portable equipment. This allowed us to refine an entirely new service, delivering Team Engagement Days in VR. It went on to account for 25% of the business' revenue for the financial year 2020/21. By being agile, we increased our own commercial resilience and thrived.

Complex Problem Solving

AI can do many things better than humans: ask it to count the stars in the known universe, and it'll do it faster and more accurately than any human; ask it to spot cancer in tissue slides – Google Health showed incredible results in 2020. But for now, it can't ask meaningful questions, which, as I've already demonstrated, is why it can't invent the meringue. That's where humans come in.

Solving problems lies at the core of innovation and intra/entrepreneurship. Problems create opportunities. Indeed, that's where jobs, businesses and organisations come from. Take climate, for example. Rising temperatures will mean water evaporates from one place, but ends up being deposited in another. That's a problem if you live in a drought-stricken area. It's also a problem to be solved. It's why we'll see more 'Water Harvesting' jobs being advertised, where creative technologists extract moisture from the atmosphere to create drinking water.

A key skill of the future will be to ask the big questions and look at creative ways to solve them.

Empathy

Empathy – our ability to understand and share the feelings of other people – will be challenging for AI to replicate in near- to mid-term future.

Yet more of the workplace relies on empathy than we perhaps realise; for example, think about human managers who are required to constantly consider interpersonal conflicts and human emotions, as well as the practical skills and functions of their teams. Another interesting example is a trial lawyer – machines can't yet reason, persuade people or intuitively know the right time to introduce an argument to the opposing party. All of these traits arise from emotional intelligence.

During the Covid-19 pandemic, we saw a significant negative impact on mental health due to bereavement, isolation, loss of income and fear. Good managers were mindful and supported the emotional health of their teams, while demonstrating and encouraging healthy work habits. Empathy matters because these future shocks are here to stay: Covid-19, climate change, the Ever Given blocking the Suez Canal, war in Ukraine. Life is increasingly unpredictable, and managing a business during inevitable future shocks will without doubt require high levels of empathy.

Resilience

The World's $1 trillion per year problem; Deloitte estimates that it costs employers $2,000 per person per year.

Low resilience, triggered by uncertainty, is a recipe for mental health problems. Yet change and uncertainty are exactly what the future of work will be about. Therefore, resilience is a key skill – and one that's learnable.

At the individual level, resilience is our ability to adapt and recover quickly from challenges. At the organisational level, resilience is the ability to protect and grow value in the face of rapidly changing external conditions. The Covid-19 pandemic has been both an economic and personal test for individuals and organisations alike. How well we respond or bounce back from challenges is determined by personal, team and organisational resilience.

Future shocks and technological change will require resilience to be hardwired into the culture of our workplaces. Building resilience in the workplace means leading with empathy and awareness of how others are feeling. With that in mind, we must constantly assess what needs to change and how quickly. And finally, having the discipline to remain focused on those changes – executing them consistently, with good communication, and nurturing teams along the way.

In short, resilience will be the foundational skill for success in the changing world of work brought about by sophisticated automation.

Contingent Team Working

Organisations typically require staff to work thirty-two to forty hours per week to be classified as full-time. Full-time employment often comes with benefits that are not typically offered to part-time, temporary or flexible workers, such as annual leave, sick leave and health insurance.

Gig or contingent workers are independent contractors, online platform workers, contract firm workers, on-call workers and temporary workers. Gig workers enter into formal agreements with online, on-demand companies to provide services to those who need them. Unlike traditional employment norms, 'employers' are loosely those with tasks that require completion; 'gig workers' are those that seek to complete them.

Gig workers run the gamut of skill levels, ranging from taxi drivers to data scientists. That said, some industries attract more contingent working than others. The most popular industry for gig working is arts and design, where around 75% of workers in the US are freelance.

Covid-19 accelerated the growth of the gig economy as firms faced headcount freezes. They needed work done, but were reluctant to renew full-time contracts. On-demand labour also addresses the widening skills and talent gaps we explored earlier in 'Continual Learning' on page 51 – if a company can't find permanent talent, why not rent it by the hour?

Taking the US as an example, in 2018, the gig economy was worth roughly $204 billion, but that number is expected to reach at least $455 billion in 2023. It's a growing megatrend and one you need to be aware of. Some studies even forecast that the number of 'giggers' will outnumber those in traditional employment arrangements in the US by 2027. Whatever the measure, full-time employment is in terminal decline and contingent working is in the ascendancy.

Creating the Contingent Team

In the office, teamwork demands **interpersonal trust** – perceiving that others won't harm your interests. Without this trust, the workplace cannot function effectively to achieve its goals. This is built through social interaction and collaborative working.

Being hired and rehired in a task environment is about demonstrating your **task-based** trust, which is why reviews from previous clients and maintaining a credible reputation are crucial in the gig world, especially for securing repeat work. It's not just the work you produce, it's also how you work with people. If the flexibility of gig working attracts you, here are two guiding principles to thrive:

1. **Be reliable**

   Keep your word. If you agree on a deadline or make an appointment to call a team member, keep your word. Demonstrating integrity and a work ethic will show you can be relied upon.

2. **Be consistent**

   Maintain that reliability, and all the other characteristics you value, time after time. Some employed people can rest on their laurels and do just fine; in the gig world, you're only as good as your last job.

Conversely, when building a team of giggers, consider how you also respect their rights – they may not have the same employee benefits as the rest of your employees, but they are a valuable part of your team and can be crucial to the success of a project. Therefore, ensure that they feel valued. Think about how you also need to build their trust, through giving accurate briefs, communicating changes, respecting their time and work boundaries and treating them ethically.

Gigging for a Living

The early promise of the gig economy was a win-win for everyone. Digital enablement meant that drivers could work the hours that suited them; restaurants would not be required to increase head-count to make deliveries. Things ran smoothly for a few months – until the app updated; the pay formula changed and many drivers found themselves out of pocket – and angry.

Then, August 2016 saw the first London strike by gig workers. The demonstration was the result of immense creativity behind the mobilisation of a large group of people. Delivery riders used a combination of Facebook and Twitter posts to gain traction amongst colleagues. What was really interesting, though, was the way in which protestors ordered food deliveries – on the platforms against which they were objecting – in the location of the protest and so were able to persuade fellow workers to join, even when they had no prior connection with those riders. A subsequent protest in 2018 made national news and succeeded in securing a commitment from the company of 'minimum payment guarantees of £9 to £11 an hour'. This is a great example of precarious workers with no tangible employment rights fighting back against a multi-billion-dollar company with seemingly unlimited resources.

Nevertheless, gig working is not for everyone, there are distinct pluses and minuses:

Advantages	Disadvantages
You can decide on the jobs you apply for and take.	You're typically only paid for the work at the point of completion.
You can decide where you work from and what your schedule is.	You could find yourself competing against 'taskers' in countries with lower costs of living. That means lower pay.
Once you've created a strong reputation, you'll have better offers that suit your work–life balance.	Working from home on a laptop can increase the sense of loneliness.
A McKinsey study found that independent workers who do it by choice and as their primary income source report higher levels of job satisfaction than traditional employees.	If you're someone who likes structure and guidelines being set for them, gig working may not be for you. It requires a high level of discipline.
You can find yourself part of a wider variety of short-term projects, continually building experience in a range of contexts.	You will need strong resilience, especially while building your reputation in a competitive online market

Regardless of whether you're on the buyer or supplier side of online labour platforms, something to watch for is increased worker rights. In the UK there is now a Director of Labour Market Enforcement appointed by the government to lay the groundwork and set up a single enforcement body for workers' rights in the UK.

With more platform work, comes more algorithmic management and worker surveillance (people managed by computers). Unions are getting involved to help ensure workers' rights aren't being eroded in the name of productivity. Indeed, the Institute for the Future of Work is proposing an Accountability for Algorithms Act, which would ensure management algorithms are used in a fair and transparent way. Moving forward, expect to see more trade unions making data a part of their bargaining agenda.

Whether you view contingent working as an opportunity or a threat, it isn't going anywhere and it is inevitable that future teams will be made up of both full-time employees and gig workers. To make these collaborations work, it will be essential for everyone to understand and respect their role and ways of working.

Creativity and Originality

When I was at school, I was told that I was not creative. I couldn't draw or paint with much talent and my work with clay usually ended up making ashtrays of different shapes (I've long since nailed the smoking demon in its coffin, by the way). It was out of school that I began to understand what creativity actually was – mainly through organising events, gigs, parties and even learning guitar to play in a band for a short while. I learned that creativity is really about finding new routes between problems and solutions. I've also learned throughout my career that everyone is creative: we can all innovate – given time, freedom, autonomy, some experience to draw on, perhaps a role model to emulate and the motivation to get on with it.

Creativity and originality matter. For now, they are uniquely human characteristics that differentiate us from the machines handling our systematic, repetitive work (although the World Economic Forum forecasts an AI could write a *New York Times* bestseller by 2049. My sense is this could be much sooner).

I'm convinced that future success involves combining creative, social and technical skills. We'll find immense opportunities and be highly resilient to future automation.

For example, legal work isn't usually seen as a creative occupation. In the very short term, basic tasks, including document analysis and document drafting, will be handled by AI. Lawyers of the future will instead develop systems that solve clients' problems. This will include design thinking and working across multifunctional teams to create new client solutions.

There is plenty of room for this creativity, for example:

> » New processes, e.g. developing smart contracts for block-chain applications, which are rapidly becoming accepted as repositories of truth. Consider a blockchain that enables healthcare records to be shared automatically when a patient develops new disease symptoms.
> » Entirely new forms of legal precedent – commercial space law, for example.

All of this can be done with the support of AI technology, which will handle the drudgery, while legal professionals focus on the cutting-edge creative solutions.

THE FUTURE OFFICE

Ultimately, it is the synthesising of all the skills we've discussed that will create the future-ready teams of tomorrow, but tomorrow's workplace isn't just going to be impacted by AI – there a host of other issues and trends that will direct on our office lives over the forthcoming decades.

Perhaps one of the most obvious changes to the office as we once knew it, is that it is no longer the hub of the workplace. Emerging from the Covid-19 pandemic, where we work is less likely to be a single place and our teams are more likely to be spread over multiple locations – working together remotely.

Home and Hybrid

According to research from International Workplace Group, 72% of office workers would prefer long-term flexibility about where they're based over extra money. Additionally, two-thirds of applicants wouldn't bother applying if a job didn't feature hybrid working. The research even went on to state that employees would rather have the option to work remotely than receive a 10% pay rise. Interestingly, survey data from a 2021 study from the UK's Office for National Statistics found that 85% of adults who worked from home during the pandemic would want to divide their working time between home and the office – showing that it's not a case of completely ditching the office.

So, did the largest homeworking experiment in history negatively impact productivity? Not really. Indeed, many reported they were more productive. CIPD (Chartered Institute of Personnel and Development) research pointed towards 7 in 10 employers reporting a **net increase in productivity** during the pandemic. Accenture's 2021 'Future of Work' study found that 63% of companies with 'high-growth' characteristics have enabled 'productivity anywhere' workforce models. That was in contrast to the 69% of firms with negative or no growth remaining fixated on where their people worked. All of this evidence tells us remote work is both desirable and good for business.

Survey data from Randstad indicates that 78% looked forward to returning to the workplace (albeit not necessarily full-time). Yet, with so much focus on sustainability, less commuting will be good for the planet. Any employer offering hybrid working is boosting its sustainability credentials. By cutting the number of commuter journeys, there's an obvious correlation with cutting carbon footprint. And this is quantifiable, as employers will have access to staff travel records by knowing who's in the workplace on a given day.

Employers will need to recognise that a one-size-fits-all approach won't work with hybrid working. Home working and lockdowns enabled employees to have their own realisations about what works for them and what doesn't. As shown earlier, many are more concerned about a flexible work policy than a pay rise. That speaks volumes about the permanent behaviour and mindset change caused by Covid-19. The 2021 Covid-19 Working from Home survey conducted by Professor Phil Taylor and colleagues consulted 3,000 people and found the following:

» 78% of respondents would prefer to work in the office two days or fewer each week
» 31% of respondents stated they would prefer not to spend any time in the office

During the pandemic, many employees experienced greater **autonomy** and discretion over their working lives. With less direct management control and no requirement for presenteeism (being present at a physical workplace), added to which the discretion on when to work, where to work, when to take breaks and how to organise tasks, were all big pluses.

Many employers felt the benefit of this through a **productivity** dividend. Consulting firm Mercer reported that 94% of employers found that productivity was as high or higher following the shift to remote working.

While Covid-19 didn't bring about hybrid working, it accelerated a dramatic and permanent evolution towards it. It's also fair to say that younger workers and digital natives were particularly comfortable with it, given their familiarity with the technology that's enabled the shift.

Forward-thinking companies will come to see the merits of a 'third space'. Somewhere that's neither the HQ nor the home. These locations will aim to remove the distractions of homeworking while freeing people from the rat-race of HQ life. Therefore, expect to see further growth of flexible and co-working spaces for hosting meetings and encouraging networking. International Workplace Group are an example of a pioneer in this area, having signed a deal with Japanese telecoms operator NTT in March 2021. Not only does the deal secure access for 300,000 NTT staff to access 3,400 'flexspace' locations globally, but an app is now in place to help employees find one another at these locations.

Productive remote work is possible because of a digitised, IT-enabled world. It's easy to share and consume quantitative information like sales revenues and financial data across all stakeholders. And using the wide range of technology at our disposal (emails, websites, newsletters, social media) is essential to get information out in a timely manner.

However, it's the hard-to-quantify, tacit information that's not easy to measure or transfer. Honesty, understanding and satisfaction are still best gauged in face-to-face situations. It's the body language, paralinguistic and auditory cues that are harder to pick up in the virtual world.

As offices reopen for hybrid working, we'll hear more about so-called '**proximity bias**'. Proximity bias is the notion that employees with physical proximity to their team and leaders are perceived as better than remote-only workers and will experience greater workplace success. It manifests as on-premise workers getting better perks and more time with executives. Some remote workers get left out of meetings and paid less than co-located team members. With the associated administrative nightmare, some experts say it's time to get rid of offices altogether.

Learning to navigate a world of hybrid work while avoiding proximity bias will be rocky, both for employees and employers alike. For example, some organisations offer childcare at the workplace as a perk. In a hybrid world, will they need to offer a separate stipend for the same thing, but for employees working at home? According to Darren Murph, Head of Remote at Gitlab, a 1,300-person all-remote workforce:

'becomes this administrative nightmare, and that's just one tiny example that proves the point … And wherever the execs are, that's where the power is going to be. Getting rid of [all] the offices ensures a more equitable type of environment.'

It's obvious that working life won't go back to 2019 business as usual. Too much has shifted. At its heart, a successful hybrid workplace revolves around trust. Employers who want to retain top talent will need to develop strategies that trust employees to choose where and how they work. Getting hybrid strategies right will require experimentation around both flexibility and creating a new form of workplace culture that fosters human connection with networking and development opportunities for those who seek it out.

From Blockchain to Metaverse: The Workflows and Interfaces of the Future

You've probably heard of the blockchain in association with the original cryptocurrency, Bitcoin. Indeed, it's the underlying technology that makes Bitcoin possible; as Don Tapscott says:

'The blockchain is an incorruptible digital ledger of economic transactions that can be programmed to record not just financial transactions but virtually everything of value.'

In simple terms, blockchain is a decentralised database. Rather than data records being stored on central servers, the data is copied and stored across a network of computers. The benefits are that records are uncorruptible and transparent – there are no middlemen and so trust is hardwired into the network.

Blockchain applications will impact the products and services we use and, therefore, inevitably impact the way we work as well.

Sharon O'Dea
Co-Founder
lithos.partners

Unbundling jobs in the multi-generation workforce of the future

Work is becoming disconnected from place, from time, from balance sheets and, increasingly, from human labour.

The logical endpoint of these trends is the decline of 'jobs', where individuals have a long-term contractual relationship with an

employer. Reid Hoffman, best known as LinkedIn's co-founder, argues that the world is in transition from a status quo of lifetime employment to one of 'temporary, sporadic and informal' work performed on a project-by-project basis.

This presents a challenge for governments, as current social and economic policy is centred on creating and taxing work in the form of jobs.

However, this shift could open up opportunities to those currently excluded from them, such as carers, older people and people with disabilities. As working lives get longer, work must be juggled with caring responsibilities and declining health, as well as repeated re-skilling.

The 'unbundling' of jobs could refranchise those lost to employment.

Web3 could underpin a new framework for work in our ageing, multi-generational workforce. We must find alternative ways of coordinating and mobilising people, assuring identity and holding immutable records of experience, qualifications and work delivered. Unbundling jobs could open up opportunities, enable coordination with the social safety net, while providing flexibility in the labour market and access to skills.

1. Finance

In 2022, there's already a mushrooming of so called 'De-Fi' taking place. That's short for Decentralised Finance. In short 'banking, but without a bank'. Platforms like Crypto.com facilitate users to save, lend, trade and hedge cryptocurrencies, all of which takes place on the blockchain. And Crypto.com is a company going places. The previously named Staples Center sports stadium in Los Angeles is now the Crypto.com arena.

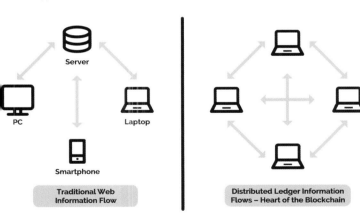

Traditional Web Information Flow

Distributed Ledger Information Flows – Heart of the Blockchain

2. Real estate sector

Some products and services simply could not exist without a blockchain to act as their foundation. Companies like RealIT let property owners 'tokenize' ownership, then sell it in fractions to multiple owners. Thereafter, the rent collected is divided amongst the investors based on their share of the property. This type of fractionalised investment/ownership could prove a boon for developers in a sometimes illiquid real estate market.

3. Supply-chain management and logistics

Blockchain is an obvious use case in this sector. Manual and paper-based records will give way to the increased trust brought about by more transparency, traceability and reduced cost associated with blockchain systems. One example of blockchain in action is Tradelens. It was founded by IBM and Maersk, and has been available commercially since late 2018. It acts as a neutral and open-trade ecosystem. At the time of writing, it had 150 members, including the largest logistics firms in the world, plus ports and terminals, ocean carriers and government authorities.

Ultimately, blockchain eases the business-as-usual workflow but removes the previous intermediaries or facilitators. For example, any traditional transaction or legal agreement requires an intermediary – someone qualified, certified and usually highly paid, who ensures that records are kept, contracts are enforced and transactions are completed. This can make such processes time-consuming and costly for the parties involved, and often acts as a bottleneck to progress. Traditionally, these facilitators were an essential part of the process – there were no transactions without banks, no contracts without lawyers, no accounts without accountants.

Blockchain could revolutionise these processes by eliminating the need for intermediaries. The immutable nature of the information stored in blockchains means that issues around trust, accuracy, authentication and enforcement are removed. This will transform the way businesses, employees and freelance workers deal with each other, while reducing the time and cost dramatically.

At an organisational level the affects could be profound, moving more companies towards a Decentralised Autonomous Organisation (DAO) model. A DAO is an organisation represented by rules encoded as a transparent computer programme, controlled by the organisation members, and not influenced by a central government. As the rules are embedded into the code, no managers are needed, thus removing any bureaucracy or hierarchy hurdles.

Bitcoin itself is widely considered to be the first fully working DAO. It has programmed rules and functions without intermediaries processing transactions, operating with a consensual protocol that prevents any single entity from controlling it.

DAOs have had a mixed reputation, including a significant trust failure when German start-up Flock.it attempted to create a decentralised version of AirBnb. Its crowdfunding campaign raised over $150m worth of the cryptocurrency Ethereum, which indicated real interest from investors. Unfortunately, a weakness in the Flock.it code was exploited within a month of launching the campaign: $50m of Ethereum was syphoned off by hackers, which undermined trust in both DAOs and Ethereum itself.

DAOs are different to traditional organisations because of something known as a 'smart contracts'. These are essentially a series of computer programmes that record transactions and execute actions based on pre-defined rules. That might include sending a financial transaction once a set of conditions are met. An example being trading stocks and shares. For example, a specific asset reaches a pre-defined price point, then the DAO purchases or sells the asset. No single individual can edit the smart contract without all other DAO shareholders noticing, which ensures the DAO remains transparent and open.

To be fully functional, DAOs need a set of rules to which they operate; a funding, like tokens, which can reward activities for members; and a mechanism that provides voting rights to establish the rules by which the organisation functions. One challenge yet to be overcome is if a fault is found in the early coding, it can't be corrected until voted on by the majority.

Compared to traditional businesses, DAOs are fully democratised by default. Subject to the DAO's structure, all changes require a vote before implementation. Most funding for DAOs nowadays comes from crowdfunding using the tokenisation principle outlined above. Governance of DAOs comes from its shareholder community. This is entirely different from traditional businesses, where decisions are reached by executives, boards of directors and active investors. The operations of DAOs are transparent and global, whereas the operations of traditional businesses are only known by the people on the inside.

At the time of writing, DAOs are still very experimental. One example is the Saint Fame web fashion house. Stake owners bought $FAME tokens and assigned a fashion designer to make a shirt and afterward endorsed the design before the shirt went on the market for sale. In this way, it comes to be a collective decentralized fashion house. Clients can reclaim $FAME tokens for Saint Fame items.

In the future workplace, DAOs are worth paying attention to. With advances in AI, DAOs could have more sophisticated rules executed by machines. Added to which, they could turn to gig economy platforms to find humans to do the tasks that cannot be executed by the programme itself. If you thought algorithmic management in the form of the app-based services like Uber were a thing, you ain't seen nothing yet!

In this way, blockchain could completely alter the structure of the workplace – changing the way we have seen teams and roles for decades. Whereas other tech advances will change the very way we see ourselves.

On 28 October 2021, Facebook CEO Mark Zuckerberg announced the renaming of the company to 'Meta'. While his motivation was questioned, it was a significant step in the growth of 'Spatial Computing'. Spatial Computing is defined as 'human interaction with a machine through digitisation of objects and spaces'. His ambition was to transition Facebook away from a two-dimensional social-networking experience to a reality that can be touched and felt: the metaverse. The metaverse isn't new. 'Second Life' from 2003 is widely agreed as the first attempt at a metaverse platform. It incorporated many aspects of social media into a 3D world of users represented as avatars. Both Minecraft and Roblox are also seen as metaverse-based social gameplay systems as well.

Nevertheless, what Zuckerberg demonstrated was what the world could look like with virtual and augmented reality as part of our daily human lives.

The shift to metaverse applications is far beyond Facebook's ambitions. It has the potential to be a world that allows all of us to be the best versions of ourselves. Opportunities for experimentation in metaverse environments is huge. People will have a chance to express themselves in ways they may not have felt brave enough to do in real life. If we can try on different 'skins' in the metaverse (expressing our sexuality in new ways, for example), it may help us hold onto new confidence in real-life environment. The real goal, therefore, is that we bring that confidence back to our physical lives. If we learn to express ourselves more deeply, it will allow people to bring more of themselves to the workplace.

A wonderful symptom of building confidence through self-expression could be a more accepting and tolerant work culture. Just imagine the positive impact on building diverse teams naturally and without mandate. That said, a significant challenge to cultural acceptance is unconscious bias.

> **Unconscious (or implicit) bias** is a term that describes the associations we hold outside of our conscious awareness and control. Unconscious bias can have a significant influence on our attitudes and behaviours, especially towards other people.

With the ability to switch avatars in a metaverse environment, biases could melt away as people come to realise that someone's 'skin' only reflects a fraction of who they are.

The metaverse also offers the possibility of enabling work to feel more like play. How about transporting yourself to a meeting with a customer based in Brazil, followed by a team meeting in the Maldives? And in the afternoon, you meet a customer at a digital twin of one of their factories to discuss new tooling? Moving between new environments will add some flair to the day and, unlike a photo or video background on a Zoom call, we'll be fully immersed into each environment.

Metaverse environments have the potential to revolutionise the way we interact with machines and one another. If the promise one day meets the hype, our working lives will look very different. Pay attention!

A Diverse and Inclusive Workplace

As a science-fiction fan, I loved *Star Trek*. Its creator, Gene Roddenbery, was an optimistic futurist. The series could be described in one word: 'hopeful'. Alongside space exploration, it depicted racial and cultural harmony amongst the crew. Did you know that Martin Luther King told Nichelle Nichols, the black actor who played Lieutenant Uhura, that he was her biggest fan? Uhura was joined by the legendary Japanese actor George Takei, who played the helmsman Lieutenant Sulu of the fictional starship USS Enterprise. According to current executive producer Alex Kurtzman:

'Gene Roddenberry's greatest contribution to the conversation of diversity in the future is that diversity is never addressed in Star Trek.'

He's right. What strikes me most about *Star Trek* is how the central characters focus on innovation, exploration and becoming the best versions of themselves. It is nothing if not about aspiration, depicting a future where humans could overcome prejudice, continuously learn and, ultimately, expand their consciousness. In many ways, those are the themes of this book.

Unfortunately, there's a way to go before we achieve the *Star Trek* utopia. However, more and more companies are galvanised to address the importance of diversity, equity and inclusion (DEI) as vital to the health of their workplaces. DEI refers to the following principles on which companies should be aligned to ensure their success:

» **Diversity:** The presence of differences in a given setting. In the workplace, that can mean differences in race, ethnicity, gender, gender identity, sexual orientation, age and socio-economic class.
» **Equity:** The act of ensuring that processes and programs are impartial, fair and provide equal possible outcomes for every individual.
» **Inclusion:** The practice of ensuring that people feel a sense of belonging in the workplace. This means that every employee feels comfortable and supported by the organization when it comes to being their authentic selves.

(Taken from Builtin.com)

DEI will be central to an organisation being considered a 'good place to work'. While many companies and individuals have sought to address issues around diversity, equity and inclusion in their workplaces, a 2018 McKinsey study highlighted the importance of embedding DEI into the office culture by showing that diverse companies had 43% higher profits. Younger generations of employees and consumers will demand this new normal. DEI themes also feed into the environmental, social and governance criteria, which are increasingly seen as an important performance benchmark for investors.

Consideration of DEI will be central to an organisation being considered a 'good place to work'. Many companies and individuals have sought to address DEI in their workplaces, and this is not just for the benefit of employees. A 2018 McKinsey study showed that diverse companies had 43% higher profits. DEI themes also feed into the Environmental, Social and Governance criteria which are increasingly seen as an important performance benchmark for investors.

Younger generations of employees and consumers demand strong, authentic DEI credentials, whether they are customers or employees. In the US (and many other countries in the Global North), each generation is proving to be both more diverse and equity-conscious than the last. A 2017 survey in Brazil found that 79% of Generation Z (born 1997–2010) will cease buying from a company they perceive to be homophobic or racist, for example. Similarly, 40% of Millennials (who will be the dominant demographic in leadership by 2025) have turned down a job because an employer didn't feel inclusive enough. This younger talent pool also values diversity (of opinion as much as race or gender identity) as a component of general wellbeing.

How businesses approach and capitalise on DEI remains up for discussion. As we enter times of economic instability and change, many companies recognise a growing skills gap and are

incentivised to work harder to attract the best talent, meeting their DEI expectations and benefiting from hiring diverse talent in diverse geographies.

Conversely, the politicisation of diversity means some firms have sought to ban discussion of DEI and politics more generally in order to avoid tension in the workplace. This may mean that DEI is at risk of being seen as less mission-critical, especially in the light of other pressing concerns: recession, economic inequality, supply chain challenges, workforce availability and climate change.

As ever, the answer will likely be to follow the money. At the moment, most businesses see real value in a diverse, tolerant, less hierarchical and more equitable culture. It's working for their operations and their brands.

The analysts agree: a Forbes study found that inclusive teams make better decisions 87% of the time; and those diverse teams deliver 60% better business results. In part, those results come from increased innovation, which is a proven by-product of a more diverse workforce. A study from Boston Consulting Group, meanwhile, with 171 Austrian, German and Swiss businesses, showed a clear correlation between diverse teams and profits from innovative products and services. Even more interestingly, innovation performance increased significantly when more than 20% of leadership positions were held by women.

THE WORKPLACE – HACKER HINTS

The following questions serve as hints for concepts you might want to ponder further to get future-ready.

Jobs arise because society has problems

Questions to ask yourself:

» Is your – or a loved one's - job open to automation in the near future?

» How might the impact of AI on the job market affect economic inequality?

» What's your view on a Universal Basic Income?

» What steps can you take now to prepare yourself for working alongside AI technology?

Upgrading our human skills for the AI age

Questions to ask yourself:

» What new skills do you think will be important for you to develop?

» What steps can you take to continually learn and update your skills?

» What platforms and opportunities exist for you to update your skills?

» Does your organisation attract talent by providing learning opportunities?

» Do you feel tech savvy? Do you feel like you have the flexibility of attitude to handle these emerging changes?

» Do you understand the importance of a 'synthesising mindset' in the AI age?

» Do you have a sense on how to develop your own synthesising mindset?

The post-pandemic workplace

Questions to ask yourself:

» How has the Covid-19 pandemic influenced your remote and hybrid work arrangements?

» What are the benefits of hybrid working to you? And what are the drawbacks?

» Is your employer providing the flexibility you need? Are there things you could do to better succeed in the hybrid workplace?

» Have you considered a co-working space? Is it right for your situation?

» Do you get the balance of technology and face-to-face interaction right?

» How can you foster honesty, understanding and satisfaction in a digitised, IT-enabled world where quantifiable information is easy to share but hard-to-quantify information is still important?

Blockchain, DAOs and the metaverse: pay attention!

Questions to ask yourself:

» Do you understand decentralisation, and how it relates to blockchain technology?

» Do you understand DAOs, and how they work through smart contracts?

» Can you see how DAOs could apply in your work/industry?

» Do you have some understanding of the metaverse?

» Have you tried a metaverse environment yourself?

» Could a metaverse environment add value to your work?

DEI is the key to long-term business success

Questions to ask yourself:

» Why is DEI important for organisations?

» What are the different dimensions of DEI for you? Is it incorporated in your workplace?

» Is your workforce diverse? If yes, do you think it leads to better outcomes?

» Does your organisation ensure equity and inclusion in its policies and practices, and do they see why it matters for long term success?

» What steps does your organisation take to attract and retain diverse talent from different backgrounds and cultures?

THE LEADERS

As digital transformation continues to impact every aspect of our lives, it's important to remember that it doesn't happen in isolation from humans. We are the ones who manifest technology and we have a symbiotic relationship with it. We live in a computerised and humanised world. It's not one or the other. Therefore, leadership needs to reflect that symbiosis – leaders not only need to lead teams of people, but also need to take the lead in how their teams work with technology to ensure that they are optimising the people and technological resources they require.

THE TECHNO LEADER

AI and analytics are impacting almost every aspect of our daily lives. However, a lot of us may not have seen this yet in our work lives. That's changing. Already the time and effort of low-skilled workers, such as food delivery and taxi drivers, are being managed by apps. 'Algorithmic management' will automate more of what human managers have previously directed, freeing up leaders to focus on more strategic-level change, such as making organisations more agile and forecasting shifts in the business environment.

For leaders, technology is both a blessing and a curse. The Internet of Things, Robotic Process Automation, 3D printing, blockchain, AR and VR will make delivering products and services both faster and cheaper. With AI's help, aspects of the delivery of those products and services will happen more autonomously (and therefore more efficiently and probably more cost-effectively). That's the blessing.

The curse is that leaders need to introduce these technologies rapidly. Failure to do so will mean being left behind. Customers have more options than ever – and can therefore expect their needs to be met quickly and for the lowest possible price. If you don't meet customer expectations, they'll just move to someone who will.

In the coming decade, AI will do most of the administrative work that takes up a lot of management time. Moreover, it'll do it faster, better and cheaper than human labour. So, how do leaders need to adapt in a world of smart machines?

1. **Let the machines do what they're good at: administration**

According to a survey by Accenture, nearly half of management time is spent on co-ordination and control tasks. For example, in many UK care homes, shift schedules are still usually arranged manually using spreadsheets. Adding in the recent pandemic, those schedules would have needed more juggling than ever, due to staff illness. Managing schedules is a task AI is particularly well suited to, and which deserves to be automated.

Creating repeated reports is similarly tedious for many of us. Since 2010, Chicago-based company Narrative Science has become synonymous with AI-powered natural language generation. Their software enables organisations to generate solid copywriting using a variety of data sources.

www.narrativescience.com

They started out by offering automated sports and financial reporting to newspapers and have now progressed to fully data-driven reporting for a wide range of organisations. Human-created management reports will certainly become a thing of the past for organisations going forward; according to McKinsey, 9 out of 10 managers would welcome it!

2. Focus on what you're good at: judgement

Google can give you a billion answers, but it can't ask a question. Forming questions and employing critical thinking is a uniquely human skill, and essential for moving up the value chain. On a daily basis, managers are required to form questions about what their teams should or shouldn't be doing next, these questions then direct strategy that needs to be informed by the history and culture of the organisation. To implement new strategy or change ways of working within an organisation successfully, leaders must be empathetic towards staff and, again, this requires emotional intelligence, not artificial intelligence. Added to this, leaders need to make

judgement calls based on an acute awareness of the wider context in which their organisation is operating. It's not enough to rely on data analysis from within the business, or even the marketplace – to be ahead of the curve, you need to have a nuanced understanding of the world around you. This is particularly true in times of socioeconomic change,

and, given the rise of sustainability agendas that are impacting all sectors, it demands leaders weigh up the ethical and economic consequences of their decisions. Applying our own experience and expertise is the essence of human judgement. That said, judgement is now informed by an increasing array of data as well as intuition. The challenge with relying solely on data is it only represents information from the past and can make us simply seek to replicate the same patterns of success or try to fix historic ways of working rather than develop new ones. Through exercising good judgement, we encourage creative thinking and experimentation, which drives our organisations forward.

3. Treat 'smart machines' as friends, not enemies

It's highly unlikely human judgement will ever be able to be fully automated. So, we needn't feel threatened by AI. Instead, we can treat it as a helpful colleague. It can analyse complex data faster and better than we ever could and thus will help us to make better decisions in our organisations. This, of course, depends on our confidence in the data we are working with in the first place, which requires us to ask robust questions about the formula we are inputting. Nevertheless, imagine being able to confidently ask your virtual assistant, 'Which materials suppliers are best placed to satisfy our needs for 2024?' and get an answer within minutes – such a working relationship

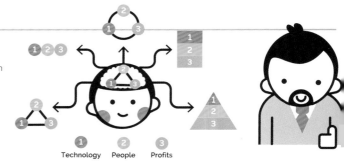

Technology **People** **Profits**

with AI would go a long way to removing some of the tedium in researching the answer for ourselves. By removing that level of granular assessment, AI enables us as leaders to move up the value chain and focus on nurturing our teams, deploying our unique human skills of empathy and creativity. For example, thinking of how we might then incentivise those materials suppliers to work exclusively with us in the year ahead or how we might co-create new materials for smart buildings over the next three years.

4. Nurture creativity in others

You're probably noticing a pattern emerge in the book. Machines are getting better at systematic, repeatable and process-driven tasks. What they're not good at is generating actual creative ideas and solutions. One way to nurture creativity across teams is 'design thinking' – an iterative and human-centred approach to solving problems. It's not just about design, but is widely used in literature, art, music, science, engineering and business. Take insurance, for example. The former CEO of Insurance Australia group was quoted saying: 'We need people who can actually layer ideas on ideas. Not somebody who has to win a competition around ideas, but somebody who can say, "Crikey! If we bring these two or three or four things together, we've got something very, very different."' Indeed, it's not hard to imagine how insurance could use the Internet of Things to reward lower premiums in return for good customer behaviour. So, good leaders need to focus more on how they can bring out the creativity within their teams, perhaps through participating

in co-learning exercises or exploring new innovations outside of their immediate sphere of responsibility.

5. Develop social skills and networks

Successfully operating at the cutting edge is one thing. We still need to bring people along for the ride. With AI executing much of the administrative and analytical work, social skills that enable coaching, collaboration and networking will make leaders stand out in a way that just 'doing the job' as we used to doesn't cut it.

$$$

Essentially, a good 'techno leader' is simply acknowledging which parts of the job could be automated and homing in on those that can't.

THE DIGITALISATION DILEMMA: HOW FAR DO YOU GO?

A productive workplace involves leaders making choices on how to deploy resources, and, as we've already explored, leaders must now think beyond material and human resources to digital ones when asking questions, such as: how do you deliver your product or service, without dropping quality or sacrificing reputation? A key trait for any future-facing leader is knowing when to deploy humans or machines to get stuff done!

Doing automation well is tricky. **Time** is a major factor in deciding whether to automate a process. How long would automation take to implement? How much time does implementation save? For

example, installing burger-flipping robots at a fast food restaurant (something which is now viable) takes real consideration. Once

installed, are they quicker than a human operator? How about the time lost when they go wrong? And they will go wrong at some point! When faced with such decisions, you need to look at the human effort in completing a task today and compare it to the benefit of your anticipated future digital state, considering all the possible scenarios.

Choosing between human resources and automation, especially in medium-sized and large organisations will require **multiple decision makers**. How many staff will you need to redeploy to make automation happen? And once implemented, will you need people to maintain the automated process?

Finally, there's the **cost**. Consider the short- and long-term costs. In the short term, it'll almost certainly be an expensive proposition, especially if you're owning (buying) rather than subscribing to (renting) the technology. With a successful implementation, and over the longer term, you'll likely benefit from lower-cost processes. From a financial perspective, will the implementation, maintenance and feasibility be worth it, or is it better to stick with the human help?

Plus, as we acknowledged in the previous section, there's an ethical dimension to consider: if automation leads to job losses – or has environmental or other social implications – how does this square with the rise of a more value-driven consumer, as well as the social imperatives of the business and its reputation?

Some emerging forms of digitalisation throw such questions into sharp relief for leaders of human teams – biometrics being a particularly obvious ethical minefield.

'Bossing' by Biometrics

For decades, we've seen biometric technology portrayed in countless science fiction films. For most movie goers, biometrics means retina scanning and fingerprints to open the doors to whatever secret facility our protagonists seek to gain entry. In the real world, it's been the preserve of the largest companies with deep pockets. However, today, biometrics means we only need look at or tap our finger on our smartphone to unlock it.

The same technology is now being deployed to unlock the doors to our workplaces, serving the same function that the 'clocking in' and 'clocking out' machines in factories of the past did. Put simply, biometrics is monitoring an employee's engagement with their work life. Identifying staff via cameras, smart door locks and computer terminals are all off-the-shelf technological solutions for authenticating identity. These biometric identification technologies now include DNA matching, ear shape recognition, finger geometry recognition and more. Back in 2002, the Defence Advanced Research Projects Agency (DARPA) investigated how a person's unique gait could be used to identify individuals. Imagine your stroll into the office literally being assessed by your biometric boss!

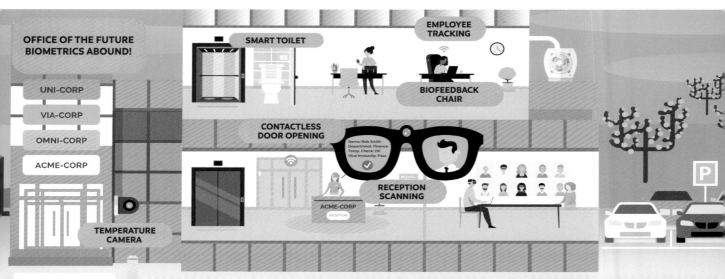

The Covid-19 pandemic accelerated a shift from millions of employees to working from home (WFH). Alongside this came advances in remote workplace surveillance. An often unfounded fear from employers was that WFH would negatively impact productivity. So, some employers introduced surveillance tools such as 'Sneek', which presents itself as video conferencing software, but also takes photos of staff at predefined intervals to ensure they are at their desks. As a leader, you need to consider whether this type of monitoring is not only intrusive, but also counterproductive, as it sends a message to people that they can't be trusted.

Biometrics also promises (or threatens) to confer physical and emotional wellbeing. Measuring heart rate, temperature and eye tracking can be used to indicate stress, anxiety and engagement. As leaders, we will need to balance the rights of our employees to privacy with the organisation's right to accurately understand how employees are feeling – particularly in relation to business change and engagement. These biometric technologies are still in their infancy, but have a wide range of real world applications. For example, where people are operating dangerous machinery, they could be scanned for signs of fatigue. In training scenarios, a course could be adapted in real time based on the emotional state of the person

taking it. More personally, biometric data could be used for health monitoring. If an employee scores well, they are entitled to reduced premiums and discounts. On the flipside, if they don't, they could risk having health insurance removed altogether. As leaders, you need to be conscious that biometric monitoring is becoming more pervasive and has real world impacts on your people. You need to be vigilant and mindful about these impacts. Before mainstreaming technologies like IoT (Internet of Things) Biometrics, it's critical to think beyond whether implementation is technically possible and to consider the following:

1. **Company culture**

   Are you as leaders willing to offer clarity and choice to employees, ultimately in service of building trust with them as they are asked to share their biometric data with the organisation? Will you be fully transparent about every use case, even if its use creates discomfort for some?

2. **Liabilities**

   You need to understand the law when it comes to collecting biometric data from employees. Precedent is still being established, so there will be grey areas to understand. If employees are members of a trade union, it will be entirely appropriate to consult with them first as well.

3. **Employees' rights and ethics**

There are the intended data uses, but what about a data breach, unintended consequences or outright misuse? Is it ethical to collect and store employee biometric data, especially in circumstances where employees feel they risk losing their jobs and income for not complying?

4. **Outright risks**

Consider scenarios where the technology fails. How disruptive to business as usual is this? Is there a fallback in place? Is there potential for fraud and misuse?

5. **Productivity gains or losses**

Does the surveillance component of biometrics increase net productivity? Do the benefits outweigh the reputational, legal and ethical risks? This remains a distinctly open question today...

Essentially, digitalisation such as biometrics is often for leaders a question of just because we can does that mean we should? Certainly, these technological shifts open up new opportunities, but in order to harness their true potential, leaders need to couple a shift in mindset with an array of so-called 'soft' skills.

WHAT KIND OF LEADER WILL YOU BE?

The Mindsets

These leadership approaches share a central idea that future leaders need to be flexible, adaptable, and open to learning and growth. They must balance the advantages of technology with the needs and values of their people and customers. Embracing diversity and global connections is key, and leaders should focus on serving and empowering others instead of just giving orders. Ultimately, they emphasise the importance of being curious, open-minded, and responsive to the ever-changing world and its challenges:

The Culinarian

A good cook knows how to balance ingredients to make great meals. Leaders of the future will balance the efficiency that technology brings with instilling purpose and wellbeing in employees. Without balancing the two, no organisation will survive, let alone succeed.

The Servant Leader

In the era of rapid technological change, it's impossible for the lone wolf leader to succeed. A servant mindset requires humility, admitting you cannot know everything and seeking to enable your teams, customers, other leaders and yourself. This is not leadership from the top down, but the bottom up – instead of determining what must be done, you're empowering others to determine the way forward for themselves. To improve your capacity as a servant leader, seek out opinions of your direct reports, develop them and cheer them on.

The Connector

Despite the trend towards nearshoring and the rise of populist politics, the world continues to become more connected. That means more globalised employees and customers. A leader who identifies with The Connector mindset will think globally and embrace diversity. As we've explored earlier, diverse teams equals more resilience, better innovation and profitability. To achieve these benefits, leaders need to be comfortable connecting and leading diverse (and often contingent) teams, using their knowledge to succeed in the global marketplace. An example of a connector in action could be staging a company or departmental event which includes a learning and social component. That way, you enable diverse participants a chance to come together while offering more than one modality (and reason) for doing so.

The Discoverer

Like Marco Polo or Christopher Colombus, future leaders will need to embrace the unknown. They will remain open to ideas and willing to change strategy as the world evolves. If the Covid-19 pandemic showed us anything, it's that organisations willing to change were those that thrived! One way to improve your discoverer leadership mindset would be to try something new. How about taking your team to a virtual reality arcade, for example? (I would say that!)

The Skills

The main idea behind these future leadership skills is that leaders should be adaptable and develop a wide range of abilities. Keeping up with the latest technology and being digitally fluent is essential. It's important to have emotional intelligence and to show vulnerability, empathy and self-awareness in order to build trust with diverse workforces. Rather than taking credit for their team's work, leaders should act as coaches, nurturing and building confidence in their team members. Having a basic understanding of futurism will be helpful to consider different scenarios and possibilities. And, honing listening and storytelling skills will help create a shared understanding and connection with their team and customers:

The Soothsayer

I'm not suggesting you need to be Yoda, but you will need a grounding in futurism. Of course, you can hire people like me to help you build a picture of the way the world is changing but you should be able to think through different scenarios and possibilities. It's not as hard as it sounds. At minimum, follow a few futurists on social platforms and subscribe to their newsletters.

The Coach

Rather than instructing teams and treating them as mere workers, you'll need to engage teams as individuals. This means letting go of the leadership ego to enable the players on your team to be more successful than you are. Don't take credit for the work of the teams you lead. Instead, shine the spotlight on those that want it. This requires you to nurture and build confidence in each individual member of the team, through cultivating empathy and social connection.

TechKnowHow'er

Make a point of talking to young people, especially teenagers, about the technology they're using and what it does for them. They can give you incredible insight into the latest technologies. You don't need to be an expert, but at least have a sense of what's coming up and a bit of know-how on how you could use it for your organisation. Digital fluency is the name of the game.

The Translator

Translators are masters of communication. At a very basic level, they make inaccessible statements accessible to others. By listening to what is being said in one language, then interpreting and relaying it in another, they create a bond of shared understanding across communication divides. Deep listening and communication have always been key aspects of good leadership. What's changing now is the range of channels available and the diversity of comms across your organisation. Hone your listening and storytelling skills, even if your role is not directly in communications, consider taking a course or, at the very least, start reading good communications (journalism or literature count), so you can create those points of shared connection with your team and customers when you need to.

The Counsellor

For too long, leaders have rejected showing their emotional sides because it was seen as weak. Going forward, emotional intelligence will be critical. Developing empathy and self-awareness are essential, especially when leading an increasingly multigenerational and diverse workforce. Showing vulnerability builds trust, and empathy helps you see the world from the perspective of others. Self-awareness means developing introspection to fully embrace your strengths and weaknesses. Ego has no place here.

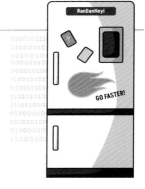

Exploring these styles of leadership will help prepare you for entirely new models of leadership that may be coming your way...

TURNING THE HIERARCHY UPSIDE DOWN

Between 2013 and 2019, I visited China several times a year for a variety of business trips. These included time at the sharp end of industrial estates in Shenzhen through to sophisticated corporate giants like Alibaba in Huangzhou. The electronics factories in Shenzhen were very traditional in how they organised themselves. Orders came in, orders came down, workers did what they were told. Alibaba showed me something different altogether. The team I worked with there was different to anything I'd seen before. They were highly self-organising and with enormous discretion over hiring, salary rates, purchasing decisions and setting their strategic direction. I'd never seen anything like it in Europe, where decision making was often slow and required layers of management involvement before any value-adding activity was allowed to start. It got me curious. Was this self-management (especially as part of a large corporate structure) something unique to China? In connection with my futures work, I started to research it. As it turned out, yes it was.

RenDanHeyi is an operating model spawned by a formerly small fridge-making company called Haier. You might even own one of their fridges. Over nearly forty years, they've evolved into one of the leading Internet of Things equipment manufacturers on the planet. What's most interesting is how they've achieved it. Their CEO Zhang Rumin is the man who conceived RanDanHeyi as a

means of driving innovation in a non-hierarchical and self-organising way. Via the Corporate Rebels website, he explains: 'We replaced the bureaucratic model with a model based on self-employment, self-motivation, and self-organization. Our goal is to let everyone become their own CEO.'

Traditionally managed corporations would be perceived as healthy if they achieved 2–3% growth per year. Since going all-in on RanDanHeyi in 2012, Haier has averaged 23% annual growth to 2021, with its features enabling Haier to bring full production back online by February 2021, and to maintain growth, even as the Covid-19 crisis forced others to contract.

Although there's much talk in Western business about the need to break down silos and enable collaboration, the sad reality is that these are unfortunate symptoms of a command-and-control leadership style that developed during the Industrial Revolution. And, in the era of mechanical machines and engines, dividing and atomising labour worked. There was a predictability about machines: designed by blueprint, interchangeable parts, all operating to standardised rules. The organisations that built them were designed in the same way, with fixed bureaucracies driving siloed functions to keep building more machines. As management guru

Gary Hamel once said on bureaucracy, 'it saps initiative, inhibits risk taking, crushes creativity and is a tax on human achievement.'

The twenty-first century is quite different. It's an age of uncertainty, rapid technological change, with everything and everyone interconnected, internet-enabled communications and, increasingly, IoT devices that enable objects to talk to themselves and to us via the network. Today's working generation are better educated and skilled than any preceding them. Given this, organisations will need a more 'Haier'-type approach to deal with future shocks, such as the long-term impact of the Ukraine war, or extreme weather events arising from climate change, or a cyber attack at a scale never seen before. Indeed, Haier's self-organising 'quantum' style management technique has already proven itself resilient, innovative and a driver of incredible growth.

RenDanHeyi: Talking About a Revolution

Author Danah Zohar makes a point in her 2021 book *Quantum Management* that 'while the number of employees in large companies has increased by only 44% in recent years, the number of middle managers has grown by 100%'. RenDanHeyi advocates scrapping bureaucracy and clearing out middle managers. With this comes dispatching the notion of linear management and power cascading from the top. Haier made this real in 2012 and now there are just two layers of management between the CEO and frontline employees.

In RenDanHeyi, once the organisation is lean and agile, siloed teams and their monopolised remits get replaced with multi-functional, co-operating teams who are empowered to make decisions, take responsibility, draft strategy, conceive of new products and services, and even enabled to communicate directly with customers. Once Haier had fired its (then) 12,000 middle managers, they divided themselves into 4,000 'micro-enterprises' (MEs). The (then) fired managers were given the chance to rejoin the business as entrepreneurs running their own MEs. What's really interesting to me is that following the loss of many jobs, RenDanHeyi created tens of thousands of new ones.

In this model, leaders don't assign employees to specific MEs. They don't tell them what to do or how to comport themselves, they're not even given fixed goals. Teams are self-organising and self-selecting, and work towards long-term targets (which are set by leadership).

These MEs each have 'three rights', which map to roles usually taken by senior leadership in a traditional, hierarchical organisation. MEs have:

1. The right to set their own strategy, decide their own priorities, how to achieve their targets and what partnerships they want to make.
2. The right to hire their own employees, assign their roles and decide on co-operative relationships.
3. The right to set the pay rates of each team member and how to distribute bonuses among them.

91

Each ME is essentially a small, independent company in its own right, offering its own products and services, owned by its members, creating and communicating with its own customers. Employees are motivated to create value – especially given that many are paid directly by internal or external customers as opposed to salaries from the company. Most of you are probably slack-jawed while reading that last sentence, but it's a model that works!

On the surface, all of the above might sound like organisational nirvana to some of you. However, I've seen it with my own eyes at Alibaba, it wasn't without its downsides, too. One team member told me: 'If you're not seen to be contributing, you're just not invited to the meetings any more.' Then, of course, you've got to explain what's going on in your performance reviews. Just like in the external world, money flows to where it's seen to create value. Those teams that perform well see budgets flow towards them. Other teams will experience the sharp edge of a win-lose game, feeling the effects of internal budgets flowing the other way. It's effective, but it's also a brutal meritocracy that many traditional employees won't be familiar with. Despite the challenges, I did witness a sense of fairness in the time I saw the system play out, and the team who contracted me certainly seemed to thrive on it. I ought to reiterate that my personal experience was with Alibaba, not Haier, so I caution readers that I can't comment directly on how this model played out at Haier.

All my surface critique aside, RanDenHeyi could easily have wider applications than just profit-making business. The notion of small, independent, self-organising teams could be applied to the delivery of community services in towns and cities, local health services, even national and global infrastructure projects. Perhaps most exciting is how learning opportunities could be modernised and relevance maintained for school and university students. I particularly like the idea of enabling enterprising students to experiment with the model to create ultra-relevant learning modules for themselves and their peers.

RanDenHeyi: Resilient Leadership From the Bottom-Up

As well as potentially fostering growth, RanDenHeyi offers a possible roadmap for resilient leadership. The model asserts that people and events are not to be manipulated and controlled, for the simple reason that the world is more complex than ever. RanDenHeyi is suited to a chaotic and uncertain world precisely because of its capacity to make decisions quickly. Leadership exists to offer service, support, resources and inspiration. In other words, to become the bottom of the pyramid, supporting employees at the top.

RanDenHeyi is also perfectly placed to steer organisations in complex market conditions. For example, climate change will lead to extreme weather events that disrupt supply chains. Our reliance on technology creates new vulnerabilities. According to NCC group, ransomware attacks rose 53% between January and February 2022. Such threats could stop traditional companies in their tracks. However, the 'many hands on deck' model of RanDenHeyi enables new teams to be formed quickly and to make local decisions and alliances with external partners and customers as needed. In times of crisis, employees do look to leaders who can keep the ship steady – in RanDenHeyi that leadership is cultivated, not commanded, it is achieved through social influence. And, within Haier, the organisation is a fleet of ships rather than a single boat.

Ransomware: a type of malicious software designed to block access to a computer system until a sum of money is paid.

Given all this, RanDenHeyi is certainly a model many organisations could consider, but it is not the only way to become shock-ready. Learning how to handle shocks is perhaps the most essential skill any future-ready leader can cultivate. Those who are familiar with traditional threat-analysis models, such as VUCA (used to assess Volatility, Uncertainty, Complexity and Ambiguity) may feel that these are enough to navigate the shocks that are coming, but a new VUCA may be needed.

THE NEW VUCA

The Covid-19 pandemic has shown us just how quickly a world-changing event can bring about large-scale societal changes that all of us, including organisations and their leaders have had to navigate.

VUCA, an acronym from the 1990s US military, is now often quoted by theorists and consultants to also describe the operating environment of modern business. It's a staple of business continuity planning and for good reason. In case you've not come across it, here's what it means, with some real-world examples:

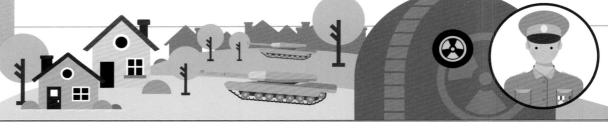

Traditional VUCA: A Threat Analysis for Traditional Businesses

Volatility: Change happens quickly and is unpredictable in nature.	An example of volatility is the way in which oil prices reached nearly US $155 in 2008, only to drop as low as US $48 later in the year. This didn't just affect Exxon and BP, but everything and everyone from car manufacturers to airlines – imagine how quick they were to rewrite their hedging contracts!
Uncertainty: The future is sufficiently unclear to make sound decisions.	In 2011, HP suffered as a result of the Tōhoku earthquake, which damaged a critical component of its supply chain. That created uncertainty as cashflows were threatened – a sentiment amplified in the markets.
Complexity: Many different, interconnected factors manifest themselves with the potential to bring about chaos and confusion, or to make unpicking cause and effect challenging.	To see complexity, take a look at how our global banking system functions. HSBC, NatWest and plenty of others are struggling as (along with other issues) consumer behaviour outpaces layers of IT infrastructure dating back to the 1970s. New high-tech 'challenger banks' are stealing a march on their legacy competitors with agile, simple and, therefore, cheaper service offerings.
Ambiguity: A lack of clarity or even awareness about situations.	Any Western company looking to do business with China will be tempted by a burgeoning middle class and its desire for Western goods. On the flip side, there's risk in parting with intellectual property and a bureaucracy which is perceived as unfathomable to Western eyes. That's ambiguity.

The traditional VUCA analysis is still entirely relevant and credible. I'm sure you can apply it directly to your own experience of running your organisation during the pandemic. However, I'd like to propose a new set of operating principles for being future-ready for the challenges that we know are coming beyond Covid-19:

Future-ready VUCA: An Optimistic Set of Approaches for Modern Businesses
(Adapted and expanded from a model put forward by Futurist Gerd Leonhard)

Velocity: Our ability to enact change quickly for shifting circumstances.	The UK's National Health Service (NHS) is commonly thought of as a lumbering bureaucracy. However, across nine days in 2020 it adapted 88,000m² of the Excel Exhibition Centre into 80 hospital wards, each with 42 beds. By partnering with 200 soldiers, contractors and NHS staff alongside, it was considered an incredible achievement. That's action with velocity!
Unorthodoxy: Staying curious and ready to approach challenges in unusual ways.	Social distancing in 2020 didn't stop the Japanese from looking for love. Dating firm Imo offered unorthodox 'drive-through meetings', where singles could introduce themselves from their cars in the empty car parks of wedding halls. Changing times are times when the unorthodox might just become profitably normal.
Collaboration: Thriving in the digital world arises from sharing knowledge and forging relationships.	As the pandemic arrived in the US in March 2020, Dealmed, one of the largest medical distributors in the Northeast, experienced unprecedented demand for PPE equipment. In response, online marketplace Alibaba.com formed a high-touch concierge service to help source protective equipment quickly. Had Dealmed attempted to do this themselves in China, it could have taken years to build the required trusted relationships. Collaboration works!
Agility: Our capacity to adapt a new mindset in order to think differently about a challenge.	Robotics manufacturer Boston Dynamics open-sourced some of its healthcare technology in spring 2020 to clinicians needing innovative health delivery solutions. By mounting tablet computers on its 'Spot' robot, clinicians in New York could interact with suspected Covid-19 patients, measuring vital signs and transporting critical supplies. In addition, Boston Dynamics made their applications vendor-neutral, so they would be compatible with other types of robotics platform. That's agility – both in thinking and execution.

Russell Atkinson,

Current CEO, Crane Garden Buildings
Formerly CEO, NAHL Group PLC

Handling the Covid-19 Pandemic

Experience has taught me that many organisations suffer from a form of institutional decision-making inertia. Over analysis, pre-conceived ideas and old paradigms slow thinking and increase timescales. Covid forced a VUCA mindset on many of us and it proved we can achieve what was previously considered 'too hard'.

For example, I was working in the legal industry and we had been investigating the possibility of flexible working and reducing office overheads for many months. It always fell into the 'too hard' category, particularly as we had a large call centre and the technological infrastructure was deemed inappropriate. However, in common with many other organisations, the situation caused us to re-evaluate what could be achieved and within two days we were up and running completely remotely. We also exited two office leases and reduced our working space significantly, forcing us to face into the issues and solve problems after taking the big decision. It was amazing how we successfully utilized a problem-solving mindset to achieve results.

Have we all learned the leadership lessons from this? Unfortunately, possibly not. I suspect that we have slipped back into the mindset of allowing perfect to be the enemy of the good.

LEADING THE NEXT GENERATION

So much has been written about multigenerational leadership already. If you're reading this, you've almost certainly come across the Boomers, X'ers, Millennials and Zoomers. What's less talked about are the Alphas – those born between 2010 and 2024. They matter, as, by 2025, they're forecast to amount to 2.2 billion people, constituting just over a quarter of the world's population. This book is geared towards life in 2030, which is when the first cohort of Alphas will be entering the workforce. Engaging them in your organisation will mean recognising that their experience of life is different to ours.

Generation Alpha

Born 2010-2024

By 2025, this generation will account for 2.2 billion people

AI AND ROBOTICS:
INTERACTING WITH MACHINES
AS FREQUENTLY AS HUMANS

CLIMATE CHANGE:
SAVING THE PLANET

DATA SHARING
HIGH DATA LITERACY.
QUESTIONING DATA SHARING

DIVERSITY, EQUITY, INCLUSION:
WORKPLACE DIVERSITY
AND INCLUSION WINS!

EDUCATION:
LESS FORMAL,
MORE SKILL BASED

HEALTHCARE:
MORE SELF-SERVE AND MENTAL
HEALTH AWARENESS. EXPECTS
WORKPLACES TO OFFER MENTAL
HEALTH COVERAGE.

MEDIA LITERACY:
SEPARATES FACT FROM FICTION.
TRADITIONAL 'PUSH' INTERNAL
COMMS WON'T WORK

Unlike previous generations, Generation Alpha will have access to information at a scale of no other before it. Even if parents restrict access to social media, their media range is well extended beyond child-centric programming. The broader influences afforded by YouTube will almost certainly bring about a shift in aspirations. They'll understand the reality of being a nurse or a scientist, as they'll have access to first-hand accounts. That matters, as they'll have a sense of pragmatism about the career paths they want to follow. They'll be tech-savvy, racially diverse and incredibly influential.

AI AND ROBOTICS:
INTERACTING WITH MACHINES
AS FREQUENTLY AS HUMANS

If Millennials were the smart-phone generation, then AI and robotics will be the technology of Generation Alpha. With the rise of voice systems and chatbots, interacting with machines will be as normal and frequent as with other human beings for Alphas. We're only at the cusp of machine interaction. Advances in AI, robotics and materials science could mean romantic and sexual relationships with robots are both widespread and normalised by 2050. The lesson for us here is not to judge the choices made by younger generations as they shape their world and how they choose to live in it.

CLIMATE CHANGE:
SAVING THE PLANET

They are growing up seeing a string of false promises and inaction on climate issues, resulting in a deteriorating world. In 2019, Wunderman Thompson Commerce found that 67% of 6 to 9 year olds they surveyed wanted to make climate change a central aspect of their future career choices. Not only will reversing climate change be core to their working lives, but the report found that over a third would only buy from purpose-driven companies and those actively demonstrating their positive environmental or social impact. To say they're values-driven doesn't come close!

DATA SHARING:
HIGH DATA LITERACY;
QUESTIONING DATA SHARING

Many of us who signed up for internet technologies such as Google Search, Facebook and Twitter had no idea about the implications of giving away our personal data. We were just grateful for the arrival of services that let us access information quickly and connected us to friends and family in new ways. Over time, society has come to understand privacy better, with more countries introducing data privacy laws such as GDPR. Generation Alpha will be more questioning, asking: '*What am I prepared to give away about myself in order to access services?*' They will be far more data-literate and, with Web 3 looking to be increasingly decentralised, they'll have more choice than ever about how to manage their data. Expect Gen A to read the fine print in your Terms of Service and to demand that the exchange of data for service is equitable. Businesses that don't respect Gen A's concern for its data will risk losing customers and audiences.

Henry Rose Lee
Intergenerational Leadership Expert
www.intergenerationalexpert.com

Tales from Gen A

In one class of thirty 12-year-olds I recently visited, one Gen Alpha said he was going to set up an online business as a kennel. No, it wasn't Avatar or SIM dogs. And No, he hasn't got a garden or anywhere to look after dogs.

Another said she was going to sell vintage clothing online (that's 1980s and 1990s clothing) because she'd seen her sister do it and make good holiday money. 50% told me they wanted to be online influencers because you 'get free stuff' and you 'travel all over the place' (climate change, anyone?).

Seven girls and two boys told me they wanted to be famous on Tik Tok for singing or dancing. Most of the class told me they would like to set up their own online business and work from home.

None of them wanted to be a fire-fighter, or chef, or dancer, or doctor, or engineer, something I used to hear when I visited schools in years gone by. Technology is brilliant in my view, but I don't believe it will suddenly give every Gen Alpha a fascinating, fulfilling job.

Yes, some video game engineers will probably love their work and may even cross over into gamification of work training, comms or performance. But most will find work less exciting and more mundane. And very, very few will be influencers or Tik Tok stars. Humans need value and a point to their lives. But who is going to teach Gen Alpha that new tech won't necessarily deliver that? Old-school education, training, work-experience, trial and error, and great human leadership probably will.

> **DIVERSITY, EQUITY, INCLUSION:**
> WORKPLACE DIVERSITY
> WINS!

In 2019, research by the Pew Reseach Institute found that 69% of surveyed participants across twenty-seven countries felt that racial diversity had increased in the previous twenty years. Gen A are growing up increasingly aware of the challenges faced by individuals around diverse issues such as race, gender, sexual orientation and religion. Both brands and the organisations they work for will need to reflect their values on diversity. It's a zero-sum situation – those that don't will simply get left behind. The same will be true for leaders of Gen A teams. No longer will leadership be awarded deference – respect and collaboration will only come through a sense of shared values and purpose. Future-ready leaders will need to start developing a clearer sense of their organisations value set in order to start attracting this new generation of workers as they emerge from the education system. Leaders will also need to take into account a new attitude to learning that will not only impact the CVs of Alphas but also how they respond to organisational training.

EDUCATION:
LESS FORMAL,
MORE SKILLS-BASED

I grew up believing that a university education was a ticket to a better life. It was almost to the point of not seeing an alternative. Of course, that was in an age where information was still restricted to the lucky few. The seeds of the internet were only just being planted. Generation Alpha will find it hard to comprehend that there was a time when people couldn't access answers to any question in seconds. Not only that, they'll be the most educated generation to have ever existed. Our World in Data reports that most countries provide at least twelve years of schooling for their populations. And UNESCO reports that every additional year of education increases a person's earning potential by 10%. Digital resources mean the traditional avenues for education are changing. With so many options, some Gen As will place lower emphasis on traditional university degrees in favour of a more skills-based approach. They will recognise the importance of continuous learning and adapt themselves accordingly. Learning systems will become more personalised to each student and the notion of two-hour lectures in the era of instantly available information will seem antiquated and inefficient. They will also be the first generation to have access to new forms of AI-assisted learning. For example, **Neurotutoring** is AI-driven adaptive learning that will analyse brain activity in real time and tailor the learning process to the mental state of a student. **Neuromodulation** will involve modulating neuronal activity in the brain while people are learning. Early research already showing improved mathematic learning and performance in young adults.

Leaders need to recognise the changing learning habits of younger generations and provide accordingly – mixing binge-worthy tutorial shorts with immersive educational experiences in both the physical and digital spaces.

HEALTHCARE:
MORE SELF-SERVE AND MENTAL
HEALTH AWARENESS. EXPECTS
WORKPLACES TO OFFER MENTAL
HEALTH COVERAGE.

Healthcare has traditionally oriented itself around our physical wellness. While that's still critical, Gen A will see two major shifts. They'll have learned from their millennial parents how to access self-serve healthcare. That includes online information, on-demand consultations and the opportunities provided by app-based preventative healthcare. Convenience and speed will be more important than visiting a doctor's surgery every time a problem comes up. They will be acutely more aware of the importance of managing their mental health and won't perceive the same stigma associated with seeking out help as older generations might have done. As leaders, this matters. There will be an expectation of employers to offer mental health coverage as part of a benefits package. Those that don't may find it hard to attract talent: underestimate this trend at your peril. This isn't just about healthcare packages though, it's also about creating a culture of care. Ultimately, leaders either create or inhibit wellbeing across the organisations they lead. Employee wellbeing will be a critical differentiator to the ongoing success of organisations. As Gen A enter the workplace, we'll need to have a new breed of 'enlarging leaders' who focus on growing and enhancing the younger generations. Enlarging leaders recognise that younger talent seeks to grow, develop and work with a sense of purpose. A good enlarging leader will recognise qualities they don't see in themselves, and even back employees who don't even see their own qualities. It's not uncommon that as long-term leaders leave their organisations wane. Enlarging leaders of the future won't have a succession plan, but a succession queue. As such, leadership will be partly measured by both the company culture and the diversity of people that are developed to follow on. Being an enlarging leader is especially important to Generation Z and A, both of whom expect their competency and character to grow during their careers.

MEDIA LITERACY:
SEPARATES FACTS FROM FICTION. TRADITIONAL 'PUSH' INTERNAL COMMS WON'T WORK

If there's one thing that's been highlighted since Donald Trump's entry into politics or the Covid-19 pandemic, it's the rise of mis-information, fake news and conspiracy theories. Generation Alpha will have the best media literacy to date. Their capacity to sort truth from lies will be underpinned by access to (and understanding of) AI-powered veracity tools. Leaders will need to recognise that traditional 'internal communication' top-down channels won't work. Anything approaching corporate propaganda or lacking authenticity will be sniffed out quickly.

Instead, to influence Gen A in supporting a new strategy will require you as a leader to connect with them on a more meaningful, personal level. That means meeting them where they are, which could include games, metaverse environments, podcasts and video. It will also be important to ensure that the tone is to influence, not to instruct – think back to those leadership styles of 'The Connector' and 'The Translator'. Additionally, Gen A will expect personalisation as opposed to blanket messaging, all of which will be enabled through the data they choose to share and the AI tools which will act upon it.

So, the future-ready leader not only needs to understand how to manage blended teams of machines and humans working in harmony, but also how to embrace entirely new attitudes to leadership.

THE LEADERS – HACKER HINTS

The following questions serve as hints for concepts you might want to ponder further to get future-ready.

Embracing AI as your collaborator

Questions to ask yourself:

» How can you adapt to the changing technological landscape and embrace AI as a collaborator in your work?
» What are your strengths that cannot be fully automated?
» How can you ensure that you have access to and confidence in the data that AI is working with?
» Are you comfortable treating AI as a helpful colleague rather than a threat?
» How can you strike a balance between technology and human judgment in your work, to drive your organisation forward?

The art of digital transformation

Questions to ask yourself:

» What are the benefits of deploying digital resources in your organisation?
» What challenges do you foresee in automating processes?
» How would you assess the potential impact of automation on human resources?
» What are the ethical implications of automation in your organisation?
» Which emerging forms of digitalisation could benefit your organisation?
» How would you weigh up the short-term and long-term costs and benefits of advanced digital transformation?
» How would you assess the human effort involved in completing a task, and what impact might this have on your decisions?
» What steps can you take to successfully navigate advanced digital transformation, and what resources or support might you need?

Leadership 2.0: the future-ready mindsets and skills you need to succeed

Questions to ask yourself:

» What are the different mindsets that effective future-ready leadership teams should possess in your organisation?

» How can 'The Connector' mindset be helpful in thinking globally and embracing diversity?

» What does it mean to you to be a 'Servant Leader'? How can this mindset empower your team members to determine their own way forward?

» How can 'The Culinarian' mindset balance efficiency with purpose and wellbeing in your employees?

» What does it mean to be a 'Discoverer'? How can this mindset help a leader to be open to new ideas and change strategies?

» What are the essential skills that effective future-ready leadership teams should have?

» How can 'The Coach' help in nurturing and building confidence in your individual team members?

» 'Soothsayers' keep an eye on your future. Do you have access to a capable futurist, either in-house or externally?

» How can having 'TechKnowHow' skills with a basic understanding of emerging technologies be useful for your organisation?

» How can having 'The Translator' skill, which is about mastering communication and deep listening, assist your leadership?

» How can 'The Counsellor' skill, which focuses on emotional intelligence and developing empathy, self-awareness, and introspection, be useful across your leadership team?

» Which mindsets and skills are personal strengths?

Haier's RenDanHeyi model: a lesson in resilience for the future of work

Questions to ask yourself:

» Would your organisation benefit from adopting a similar approach to the RenDanHeyi model?

» What would be the challenges or drawbacks of adopting a non-hierarchical, self-organising operating model like RenDanHeyi?

» What steps could your organisation take to implement a more agile, innovative operating model?

Using future-ready VUCA to prepare for the unknown

Questions to ask yourself:

» Can you imagine other future shocks that would shake your organisation in a similar way to the Covid-19 pandemic?

» How could the principle of velocity in 'future-ready VUCA' apply to your organisation?

» How could the principle of unorthodoxy in 'future-ready VUCA' apply to your organisation?

» How could the principle of collaboration in 'future-ready VUCA' apply to your organisation?

» How could the principle of agility in 'future-ready VUCA' apply to your organisation?

» Would 'future-ready VUCA' principles help you and your organisation to be prepared for future challenges as they arise?

Meet Generation Alpha: how the next generation will shape the workplace

Questions to ask yourself:

» Is your organisation ready to acknowledge the outlook of Generation Alpha on life and their career paths?

» Will your technology be compatible with their expectations?

» Will your values be shared by the next generation? If not, what approaches can you take?

» And if so, how would you demonstrate those values to attract and retain the next generation of workers?

» How will Generation Alpha's education approach impact their CVs and responsiveness to your style of organisational training?

» What steps would you take to understand and engage Generation Alpha employees in your organisation?

LIFE SHIFTS

In the 1950s, futurists forecast a post-millennial world populated by jet packs and flying cars. The future as we know it may look very different, but those baby boomers were right about the fact that our lives would be transformed by technology. Throughout this book, we've explored tech innovations that will accelerate innovation in the workplace and that will challenge and empower the leaders and teams of tomorrow. However, the shifts we'll experience over the coming decades are not limited to the world of work – they will permeate the everyday in profound ways that we need to grapple with now to ensure that we can thrive in our daily lives. This section cannot pretend to get you future-ready for everything, so I've cherry picked a few key themes to give you a sense of the seismic nature of the shifts we're about to experience.

URBANISATION

Rapid urbanisation since the Industrial Revolution has characterised our lives; even for those of us who don't dwell in the cityscape, its impact is felt in the 'have' and 'have not' that plays out between town and country across the land. In countries where vast swathes of territory are sparsely populated and their agricultural outputs are crucial to not only their citizens' survival but to their nation's standing on the global stage, the nexus of power still resides in tightly packed megalopolises. It is therefore unsurprising that the cradle of the future is to be found in our cities.

Smart Cities

Smart cities are the ultimate test laboratory for technologies that integrate with one another. When done right, they analyse data from a wide variety of sources to improve the quality of life for citizens. A modern smart city relies on AI to process huge quantities of data generated from Internet of Things sensors. Take London's Ultra Low Emission Zone (ULEZ) scheme, which charges drivers a fee for using the most polluting vehicles in the city. The fee is intended to encourage people to switch to less polluting vehicles; and its profits are used to 'improve the transport network and make London's air cleaner' according to London's Mayor Sadiq Khan in 2018. It enforces charges through a network of cameras that tie to the national police database. Vehicle registration numbers are checked to ensure payments and fines are complied with. This is just one example of the way that cities are now becoming sentient beings, using IT systems like sensory pathways to connect data, which the AI-enabled city brain processes to ease citizens' daily lives and implement policies from pollution reduction to democratic reform.

Here's a few examples of smart city features you might not have come across:

Intelligent Power:
Using smart technology and data analysis to make the way we manage electricity in cities better. By using intelligent power, we can save energy, cut down on waste and lower the amount of harmful gases we release into the air. It also helps make the power system stronger and more reliable. All of this is important because it helps make our cities more sustainable, liveable and efficient, using technology to make life better and reduce our impact on the environment.

LIFE SHIFTS

Collaborative Innovation Network:

A group of people, organisations and groups that come together to make new ideas happen. They work together, share resources and encourage experimentation and creativity to solve urban problems. The goal is to bring everyone's skills and ideas together to make progress, create new things and services, and tackle the tough challenges cities face today. This network can include government, businesses, schools, non-profit organisations and neighbourhood groups working together to find creative solutions for important issues like transportation, energy, the environment and making sure everyone has a fair shot. Self-awareness is essential, especially when leading an increasingly multigenerational and diverse workforce. Showing vulnerability builds trust and empathy helps you see the world from the perspective of others. Self-awareness means developing introspection to fully embrace your strengths and weaknesses. Ego has no place here.

Smart Care:

Technology and data to make healthcare services better for everyone. The aim is to make it faster, more effective and easier to obtain. It includes things like seeing a doctor over video call, keeping an eye on your health from home, using data to predict health problems, and using smart health devices. By using these tools, cities can make healthcare better for patients, save money and solve problems like not having enough doctors or having to wait a long time for an appointment. The big goal of smart care is to create a healthcare system that is connected, always looking for ways to help and tailored to each person's needs.

Smart Water:

Ensuring our city's water supply is being taken care of in the best way possible. By using sensors and digital systems, we can keep an eye on how much water is being used, find and fix any leaks, control the flow and pressure of water, and minimise waste. The goal is to have a water system that is efficient, sustainable and can adapt to changing needs. Plus, smart water can make the water you drink even better and help save water, too!

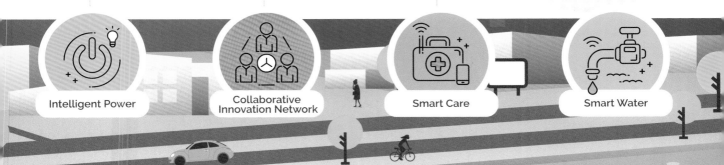

Intelligent Power | Collaborative Innovation Network | Smart Care | Smart Water

It's not just the hidden tech that makes a city 'smart' though, it's also the way in which its buildings are performing functions that stretch far beyond just offering shelter.

Yewande Akinola
Engineer and Innovator
yewandeakinola.co.uk

THE ETHOS - for our future cities.

As a designer in the built environment, I believe that the key to shaping the future of our cities lies in evolving the ethos driving its creation. In the past, various drivers like commercial wealth, housing demand and transportation have laid a solid foundation. But, there's a growing consensus among us 'creators' that we need to aim for more - our cities must serve everyone.

The term 'Inclusive Design' is driving important conversations about the purpose of our built environment and who it's designed for. It's making us question whether we're designing with children and play in mind, providing older residents with enriching facilities, and fostering transparency and security in our cities.

As we advocate for green buildings and smart infrastructure, it's essential we consider these questions. The future of the built environment will be determined by the answers we find.

The Built Environment and Biotech

With the climate crisis and a need for sustainability, it's time to think differently about our built environment. Buildings could become another part of nature. The Hub for Biotechnology in the Built Environment is a collaboration between researchers at the UK's Newcastle and Northumbria universities. Together, they are imagining buildings that grow, breathe, reproduce and, ultimately, are alive!

We already use natural materials in our buildings. Sand is used in asphalt, concrete and mortar to create foundations built for strength, bulk and stability. And, of course, wood is widely used in ceilings, walls and floors. However, a potential new material, mycelium – which forms the roots of fungi – was introduced as a state-of-the-art concept material in 2014. The 'Hy-Fi' was a concept building designed by The Living to showcase the possibility of using bricks grown from natural materials as opposed to being manufactured from finite ones. By combining a special form of mycelium with agricultural corn husk waste, the bricks were literally grown. Three months into the experiment, the bricks were composted and the resulting soil given to local communities. It is hard to say whether we'll all be living in mushroom mansions in a few years' time, but it is certain that rapid population growth is leading to a worldwide building shortage; growing our buildings could be a powerful solution and one that mitigates the many harmful outcomes of our current construction approach.

Indeed, concrete production, transport and repair is extremely energy-intensive. The Global Carbon Project estimates that it contributes around 7% of CO_2 emissions globally – that's over twice as much as the aviation industry puts out. A significant challenge with concrete in buildings is that it cracks. As cracks form, water gets in and rusts the steel structure inside that keeps the building stable. If we can make concrete last longer, we reduce CO_2 emissions – it's that simple. In 2015, researchers tried early experiments using bacteria in the concrete production process which would heal cracks and stop water from entering. However, such innovations don't come without risks; using bacteria in this way is more costly, can pose a danger to human health, it's hard to regulate and may present other structural challenges, such as fault zones.

Nevertheless, biotech and buildings are likely to remain bedfellows for some time. For example, biochemist Suzanna Scarlatta is looking at using carbonic anhydrase, an enzyme that transfers CO_2 from human cells to our bloodstream. The same enzyme can help concrete powder transform CO_2 in the atmosphere into calcium carbonate crystals, which can then fill in cracks as they appear in the concrete. This innovation could help concrete last four times longer than its current incarnation and has the added benefit of enabling buildings to draw CO_2 from the atmosphere to fix themselves. At the time of writing, the US-based Worcester Polytechnic Institute is seeking partners to commercialise the technology.

But it's not just about the way in which we build, it's also about the function buildings can perform.

Self-Healing Concrete

Buildings that Breathe

Nearly any glossy office block you visit has a series of steel lungs we call air conditioning. They're there to keep the air fresh and you from overheating, after all opening a window isn't always an option!

But the International Energy Agency forecasts that 13% of the world's electricity will be used for air conditioning by 2050, producing 2 billion tonnes of CO_2 annually.

Researchers at MIT have developed 'bioLogic': a form of synthetic skin that changes its shape in reaction to humidity and heat, allowing heat and perspiration to flow through it. In 2019, they even experimented with covering entire buildings with the membrane, which could 'sweat' as the temperature rises inside. Effectively the latex membrane behaves like human sweat glands, keeping the temperature cool for those inside. In this way, biomimicry is transforming how we look at our built environment – buildings are alive and can play a powerful role in enabling us to thrive.

One example of this in action is a building that could actively improve our gut health. In a Covid-19 pandemic world, hygiene became front and centre of the office and home. Just imagine how much money was spent on anti-bacterial cleaning products over this period. While these products help keep our homes and workplaces clean, they indiscriminately kill bacteria that's proven to be good for us. Research suggests that those who live closer to nature, on farms for example, suffer less from allergies than those in built-up areas. Now, researchers at University College London

are investigating how surfaces in hospitals could be made bio-receptive. That is to say, they would actively encourage the growth of good bacteria, helping to increase resistance against disease-causing bugs. The idea of a surface 'so clean you could eat your dinner off it' could be set to change.

These innovations aren't without their challenges. One is how to scale such technology. The second is that they are actually living. If they're alive, that means they have the capacity to die. That said, taking down existing buildings that are past their lifespan is costly, polluting and time consuming. Imaging a scenario where cities are populated with living buildings that are allowed to die, return to the soil and give birth to the next cityscape.

OUR BODIES

Biotech will bring about huge change to how economies work and societies function, as well as raise a host of global, national and personal security concerns. The revolution to come will impact us just as much as the information and communication revolutions already have. We have the potential to mitigate a range of chronic diseases such as cancer, heart disease, stroke, arthritis and diabetes.

One way we'll achieve better healthcare is through more personalised medicine.

Personalised medicine is all about giving you the right medical treatment just for you. It takes into account your unique genetics, lifestyle and health history to make sure you get the right care at the right time. No more one-size-fits-all approach! This can lead to better health outcomes, more accurate diagnoses and more effective treatments, with fewer side effects. And it's not just good for you, it can also make the healthcare system more efficient by reducing guesswork in diagnosis and treatment. Personalised medicine has the potential to change the way we think about and receive healthcare, for the better.

The human life span could expand dramatically and we will possess the ability to do away with a range of age-related illnesses. Whether that's a good thing in terms of quality of life or the resources of our planet is a separate discussion.

The 'Smart Toilet': How a Toilet Could Both Liberate and Control Us!

The flush toilet as we know it today didn't become widespread until the 1850s. Its design hasn't changed a lot since. That could all be set to change. Welcome to the world of the 'smart toilet' – and a new frontier in privacy concerns.

'Smart toilets' combine sensors and artificial intelligence to analyse our waste. By deploying sophisticated technologies, innovators believe our loos could become the ultimate health monitoring tool. Data about our waste will provide information about chronic diseases, even checking for signs of diseases, such as cancer. Aside from the serious stuff, it would give us peace of mind by showing us our healthy baseline. Biomarkers in our waste would provide us with early warnings for a check-up and tell us whether to increase or decrease existing treatments. The smart toilet could suggest lifestyle choices, for example suggesting specific classes of nutrients or fibre content. A smart toilet could be the ultimate enabler of personalised nutrition.

In 2021, Japanese manufacturer Toto announced their 'wellness toilet'. Still in the conceptual stage, its sensors would analyse scents to detect health problems and other conditions, including stress. As part of the concept, Toto visualised the toilet sending users a recipe for salmon and avocado salad. And why not – foods rich in Vitamin B3 have been linked to slowing the aging process!

However, the smart toilet can – like all technologies – be abused. You certainly know that fingerprints are unique. Well, in 2021 researchers from Stanford University partnered with Izen, a Korean toilet manufacturer, on an initiative to identify users through scanners. The scanner will recognise users through (according to the researchers) 'distinctive features of their anoderm' (the skin of the anal canal). It turns out that our '**analprint**' is as unique as our fingerprints.

Clearly this represents a privacy concern. If we can be identified through our analprint and the make-up of our waste is analysed, how can we be sure that this intensely personal data is secure? If our data is shared, what sort of organisation will have it? Once shared, can it be combined with other data; and will we have transparency as to where it goes and with whom it is shared?

Phil Booth of MedConfidential, a campaigning organisation for the confidentiality of medical records, describes a scenario whereby a smart toilet is used by a medical professional. 'There are not necessarily inherent privacy risks' in using a smart toilet, he says. However, imagine a scenario where the data created in your home was owned by a company. He continues, 'You may trust that particular company, but every company is pretty much buyable by Google or Facebook or Amazon. Then, what I thought was something for my own health monitoring has become fodder to business models I really know nothing about.'

There's already precedent for this. Remember the craze for Fitbit smart watches? Many of us bought into it, believing it to be a great tool to monitor our exercise. In January 2021, Fitbit was purchased by Google, along with all the rich data generated by

millions of devices globally. Indeed, the European Union was so concerned about the acquisition that Google agreed not to use health or location data to personalise its advertising to users. Google already has significant access to patient data in the UK and US. And if you're still wondering whether Google is interested in your toilet habits... well, it has been for a while, and even patented a toilet sensor back in 2016.

What does this mean for us? As with most technological advances, it's a double-edged sword. On the one hand, we will receive the benefit of early-stage health warnings and dietary recommendations. On the other, we don't fully understand how the product owners will use our sensor data. They're branded innocuously to us as 'smart toilets', but could easily become components of 'surveillance homes'. This type of monitoring provides information on risk of disease, diet, levels of exercise, alcohol and drug use. Even if that data isn't kept, just tracking the time we use a smart toilet could show agitated sleep patterns, which in turn might reveal an inclination towards depression or anxiety. The value of this data would be hugely beneficial to insurance companies when measuring your risk profile. More long term, if users fail to eat 'correctly', their life insurance could be voided.

That's just in the home. How about in our workplaces, where a business already has significant rights over what we do? The data

from smart toilets could be sent to HR, giving them insight into pregnancies, drug-taking and physical or mental health issues. Even more insidiously, employee healthcare plans could be tied to meeting specified metrics. For example, data indicating that employees are smokers could trigger removal from the plan altogether.

As you can see, even something as innocuous as a toilet has wide-reaching implications. Now imagine that scaled up, with dozens of devices in our homes and workplaces all generating data about us that can be filtered, correlated and analysed to profile us. As far as toilets are concerned, it's not the technology preventing it becoming a standard bathroom fixture, but the cost and our current cautiousness about the technology, but that may change. Right now, half the world's population lack access to safe sanitation. Moving out of the laboratory and conceptual phase to produce something affordable could be another ten years away, or more. We've got a while to consider the implications, but be aware, there are more than we think.

Smart toilets are just one example of how our bodies and our biology are becoming the next data privacy battleground.

Fun Smart Toilet Fact

You won't believe this, but scientists are exploring the wild and wacky idea of smart toilets that could actually generate energy! These toilets would use tiny microorganisms to chow down on the organic matter from human waste and turn it into biogas. And get this, the biogas can be transformed into electricity or even cleaned up to make fuel for cooking and heating. Professor Cho Jae-weon, an expert in urban and environmental engineering at Ulsan National Institute of Science and Technology in South Korea, has reported that the amount of faecal waste produced by a single individual in a day can generate enough biogas to power a car for 1.2km. Hundreds of little innovations like that would certainly assist the circular economy, eh!

The Ethics of Epigenetics

The field of epigenetics will influence our lives more than ever before. Epigenetics is the study of how our own behaviour and the environment and events we experience can actually alter the way in which our body reads our DNA sequence (i.e. changing the gene expression – the process by which genes are activated in a cell and start making protein, rather than the gene itself). An evolved understanding of epigenetics will explain the impact that external factors, such as diet and exercise, have on our health. Indeed, epigenetics will play a crucial role in determining the success of personalised medicine. For example, by influencing how our bodies read our DNA, there is hope of finding drugs that regulate our

113

FUTURE HACKERS

home-grown predisposition to cause cancer cells to grow and spread. Epigenetic drugs are already showing some success in stopping cancer cells from hiding in the immune system.

But every new technique comes with the possibility of either outright abuse or applications that challenge today's ethics. A highly contentious form of disease reduction is 'gene driving'. This involves using tools like CRISPR to edit the DNA of living creatures as new generations are born. A practical application undergoing research right now is an attempt to reduce the spread of malaria by mosquitoes. In 2018, a team led by researcher Andrea Crisanti edited a gene into mosquitoes kept in a cage; it stopped females from biting and laying eggs. Within twelve generations, no further eggs were laid at all, essentially eradicating that line of insects.

Other researchers are trying more nuanced versions of the technology. Omar Akbari and his team at the University of California, San Diego, are trying to build a 'trojan horse' into mosquitoes by ensuring that larvae ingest a seemingly benign crystal that releases a deadly toxin as the crystal breaks down in the larvae's gut. Such interventions require highly skilled technology and understanding of the cellular biology of these creatures, but could save hundreds and thousands, if not millions, of lives from malarial disease.

Altering the genes or biology of living creatures comes with its own set of moral questions. Clearly there needs to be more debate about the risks, benefits and values of using the technology. Is it in the interests of humanity and society?

Of particular note is the growing field of neuroenhancement, which aims to improve human performance. 'Soft' neuroenhancers encompass a range of items, such as caffeine, energy drinks, food supplements and non-prescription drugs – all of which can improve our mood, work or intellectual performance. Stronger forms include alcohol, illegal drugs and non-medical use of prescription drugs. Expect to see a new generation of scientists working on technologies that increase learning speed or combat neurological diseases such as Alzheimer's. The implications for use in the military are significant, too. Soldiers could find their awareness and decision-making skills boosted in battle. Combined with physical augmentation, such as exoskeletal frames, these mentally and physically enhanced soldiers would be formidable indeed. That said, the Jason Bourne films have shown us this enhancement could come at a cost.

When asked, the LLM (Large Language Model) 'ChatGPT' even came up with a joke about it:

Q: Why did Jason Bourne cross the road?
A: To get to the other side of his memory loss!

Biotech Gone Bad

Applications of biotech create huge quantities of data, which is continuously being examined by the Global Future Council on WEF Global Future Council and has already led to breakthrough technologies in health and medicine. That data comes from the real world: from you and me. However, often we are entirely oblivious to its existence, let alone its collection and use. There are cases where healthcare data management has gone seriously wrong.

For example, in 2015, there was a huge data breach at Anthem, a major US health insurance company. Bad actors stole personal and medical information of over 80 million customers. It included names, birth dates, social security numbers, addresses, email addresses and employment information. It was sold on the black market and used for identity theft and fraud, including opening fake bank accounts, securing loans and filing false tax returns. This had long-lasting effects on those affected, as they had to worry about identity theft and financial fraud for years.

This example demonstrates how important it is to keep healthcare data secure, and for individuals to be careful with their personal information. It also shows the dangers of cyber criminals and the importance of having strong data security measures in the healthcare industry.

We need a new way to think about data privacy. With digital health records, data from smartphone apps and cloud storage all growing, there are immense privacy risks. As our old friend AI becomes more sophisticated, so will its algorithms and their ability to identify individuals from their 'anonymous' data. What's to say that private data today isn't public tomorrow? We only need to look at forecasts for the market for the Internet of Things, which promises millions more sensors all collecting data. In 2020, the global market was valued at US$310 billion. It's forecasted to rise to US$1,842 billion by 2028 – a six-fold increase in eight years. In other words, more data means more opportunity to compromise it.

As more of our biodata gets combined, the risk of identification and breaches of privacy rises. One Harvard professor has already been able to identify over 40% of participants from the Personal Genome Project – a supposedly anonymous genetic study.

Let's look at another example of this in action. Back in 2012, a statistician named Andrew Pole worked for the US department store Target. He used information on women's buying habits to assign a pregnancy prediction. *Business Insider* even reported that a furious father turned up at one of the stores demanding to know why his teenage daughter had been sent coupons for baby clothes. It turned out Target knew his daughter was pregnant before he did!

This example may be seemingly innocuous (although perhaps not for the father and daughter involved), but such data collection will have profound impacts, especially as the drive towards personalised medicine accelerates. Advances in the field will need more patient data to be truly effective; such data will include conventional health records, but also information gleaned from sleep and mood trackers.

The questions for us are: how much of our privacy are we prepared to sacrifice for the potential benefits of personalised medicine, and how do we equip ourselves to fully understand what data is being harvested, how it is being used and what safeguards should we be putting in place?

It's not just the invasion of privacy that we need to be worried about, there is a potentially larger-scale threat: bioterrorism. Bioterrorism isn't a new phenomenon, but until now attacks have been limited in their scope. In 1993, the Japanese cult group Aum Shinrikyo tried to aerosolise anthrax from the roof of a building in Tokyo. That biological attack didn't work, but they did manage a chemical attack using sarin gas on a subway train in 1995. It killed thirteen people and made thousands of others sick. Their goal was to bring about an epidemic, which would result in a world war, allowing them to seize power. While they lacked the necessary expertise to execute the biological (anthrax) attack, it was shown that a number of their members included ex-biologists and a few had medical qualifications.

In the late 1990s, Al-Qaeda recruited biologists to help develop a programme of bioweapon development. Following the 2001 September 11th terror attacks in the US, they started sending letters laced with anthrax to US government officials. Five of the recipients died and seventeen fell sick. While small in scale, this is still considered one of the largest bioweapon attacks in US history.

The issue now is that biotechnology tools are becoming cheaper and less sophisticated expertise is needed to work with them.

Terror groups can also make use of synthetic biology to create new forms of bioweapons; for example, modifying existing pathogens to make them more virulent. For now, access to dangerous pathogens, and the tools and data to manipulate them, is very limited, but this will not be the case in ten years' time. How will nation states prepare to deal with the threat of bioterrorism? The challenge for governments worldwide is to minimise the risk and impacts of a bioweapon attack while not hampering innovation in the growing field of biotechnology.

That's not to say governments are failing to make inroads. In the US, the FBI is among a number of sponsors funding the International Genetically Engineered Machine (iGEM) competition. Essentially, this is a forum where thousands of students come together to solve pressing global issues using synthetic biology. The FBI's interest lies in building trust with participants in the competition, so that future suspicious behaviour might be reported by members. Bioterrorists usually have minimal contact with the life sciences community, but it is a start.

Staying Forever Young

'People are not living longer. They are dying longer.'
The above statement was made during a conversation with Paul Foley, a friend of mine.

Regardless of the potential for misuse, biotech is certainly here to stay and will play a huge role in saving lives; in parallel, once those lives are saved, enormous sums of money are being ploughed into an industry that exists exclusively to delay human death. In 2019, the 'prolonging life industry' was worth around US \$110 billion. By 2025, Bank of America forecasts a market value of US \$600 billion. It is entirely possible that humans will soon routinely live beyond 100. Getting us there are advances in genomics, big data, food of the future, 'ammortality' (living healthier for longer), and various moonshot medicines.

Genomics is the study of a person's entire genetic information, including all of their genes and how they interact with each other. This information is stored in a person's DNA and helps to explain differences in physical characteristics, health and disease risk. In practical terms, genomics involves analysing a person's DNA to understand their unique genetic makeup and using that information to guide medical decisions and treatments.

In 2019, a Cambridge-based researcher, Diljeet Gill, was forced to double check results of an experiment he was performing. He was testing the 'reprogramming' of human skin cells. His results showed that skin could regain its youthfulness. His supervisor reported the skin cells behaved as though they were twenty-five years younger than they actually were. This simply wouldn't have been possible without advanced genomics. That innovation led to the best-funded British startup ever, Altos Labs. Both Diljeet and his supervisor, Wolf Reik, are part of the team, alongside an array

of Nobel Prize winners. Their current ambitions aren't to enable immortality, but to wipe out age-related disease and illness: perhaps best described as increasing healthspan, not lifespan. That said, some of the funding came from Jeff Bezos and Yuri Milner (Russian billionaire and founder of mail.ru). Both are known for their public support of life-extension projects.

Big Data

Big data is important for the goal of living a longer, healthier life because it provides information that can help us understand what makes people age and how to avoid age-related health problems. By analysing data from different sources, including medical records, genetic information and lifestyle details, experts can see patterns and connections that can help them predict and stop age-related diseases. We can also make personalised health plans to help people live better, longer lives. Alphabet (owner of Google), Amazon and Apple are all very active in the field of data-driven healthcare.

Food of the Future

My personalised diet, tailored just for me by my smart food company

Future food companies are working towards creating a healthier and more sustainable food system for everyone. In part, this will involve agricultural gene editing using CRISPR-type technologies. In 2018, for example, Chinese researchers used CRISPR to create cotton plants that are resistant to bollworms, a common pest in cotton production. This breakthrough led to significant reductions in pesticide use and increased crop yields. Also, expect manufacturers such as DuPont and WW International to invest hugely in anything that supports healthier lifestyles and consumption practices. No doubt future-facing food companies will develop relationships with IoT specialists to develop health monitoring and promotion programmes. There is significant potential for profit in offering consumers personalised diets that enhance their health and prolong their lives. I only hope these diets will be accessible to all, regardless of financial status.

Ammortality

Ammortality sounds like a great idea! It's about living a healthy and fulfilling life for as long as possible, instead of trying to live forever. By focusing on our health and well-being, we can make the most of our senior years while staying active and happy for longer. And the best part? By staying healthy, we also lighten the load on healthcare systems and make the world a better place for everyone.

Moonshot Medicines

One example is the exploration of anti-aging drugs like Rapamycin, Metformin and NAD+ precursors. These medications show promise in laboratory tests for increasing both lifespan and healthspan in animals. Researchers are conducting studies in humans to determine if these drugs are effective and safe for slowing down the ageing process and reducing the likelihood of age-related health issues. This research is extremely nascent, and more study is needed before these drugs should become widely available.

I'm excited to see that the healthcare industry is making progress in enhancing human quality of life. With the help of cutting-edge technologies, such as genomics, big data analysis and advanced medicines, the goal of living healthier for longer is becoming a reality. The Office for National Statistics in the UK predicts that the number of individuals over the age of 85 will double by 2041, which highlights the importance of ethical research that supports healthy aging. Let's look forward to a future where people can live independent and fulfilling lives for longer.

OUR MINDS

Mental wellbeing has been much talked about in the last decade, and rightly so, given the statistics around mental ill health that indicate a picture of a global population struggling to adjust to the pace of change its experiencing. There are no easy fixes here and, as this book testifies, the further enmeshing of tech with our daily lives is going to present evermore challenges, along with the opportunities it brings. In order to not just survive but thrive in body and mind, we're going to need to equip ourselves with robust mental tools.

This can be achieved by not only increasing education and aware-ness, but also through the use of stress-relieving gadgets. One CEO is on a mission to reduce stress in her customers' lives:

Anna Gudmundson, *CEO, Sensate*
getsensate.com

Sensate, a ground-breaking consumer product, taps directly into the primal part of the nervous system to immediately relax people and improve stress resiliency over time. The infrasonic resonance created by a device and companion app, uses bone-conduction to target the vagus nerve. The patented hardware is a critical and differentiating factor of the non-invasive technology and its effectiveness, leading to continuous use and long-term benefits.

A majority of people regularly feel stressed and anxious. Frequent triggering of the stress response neurologically turns off the immune, digestive and reproductive functions, and our prefrontal cortex (the problem-solving, conscious and empathetic part of the brain). Most people want to break this cycle, but find meditation and other practices difficult. This type of therapy comes out of PTSD treatment and requires no practice, which is why it genuinely helps so many people.

Sensate is part of a future paradigm of frequency-based sci-ence and transhumanism. In order to evolve as society – as humanity – and to solve the burning global issues, we need to strengthen our ability to self-regulate and increase our resil-ience. Everything alive has an electrical current and therefore different frequencies. As we start to explore our world from a perspective of signals and frequencies, we open a whole new paradigm of science, medicine and technology.

Educating Generation Alpha

Education is one of the foremost of these tools, but 'traditional' education systems across the world are being stretched taut as they try to flex to meet the emerging generations' needs.

Our modern education system is only around 200 years old. Prior to it, formal education was generally something for the elites. As the Industrial Revolution changed our working style, it created a need for a universal school system. Factory owners needed willing workers who would take orders and show up on time. In other words, be willing to be a part of a larger machine. That's why 'Taylorism' (a management theory that focuses on optimising work processes through scientific analysis and division of labour to increase efficiency and productivity) has been so successful and why our education system has focused on creating **employable** people.

There's a confluence of trends forcing a need for a change in the outcomes we aspire to in our education system. As we've already explored, advances in biotech mean that we have a generation of schoolchildren who could be the first to have 100-year-long careers. Combine this with the impact of Artificial General Intelligence (AGI) handling all the systematic, process-driven and repeatable tasks, and we see why a static qualification gained in our early twenties won't be enough for long-term employability. The World Economic Forum forecasts that 65% of children entering primary school will ultimately end up working in jobs that don't even exist yet. So, how do we prepare children for a world of uncertainty and unpredictability?

In the near future, we need **adaptable** people. To foster adaptability, we need 'learnability' – the skill that helps students adapt to new situations and environments, as well as a capacity to learn new skills quickly. I'll always remember how a UK-based senior educational leader approached me in 2018 to work with his board. 'Our education system isn't fit for purpose, Matt. We're teaching as if we're in the Victorian era still,' he said. He knew what was needed, but still felt hamstrung by an outdated yet compulsory curriculum. He had the foresight to develop extracurricular activities that would enhance his students' adaptability.

Education must become more interdisciplinary and holistic in order to develop adaptability or 'future readiness'. How about

implementing **STEAM programs** that seamlessly blend ART into STEM subjects, and incorporate yoga classes that promote physical and emotional development? Let's cultivate **resilience** in students by introducing activities that help regulate their emotions and minimise negative thinking. **Self-regulation skills** need to be developed by teaching goal setting and engaging in fun, educational games in the classroom. And, to help kids **prevent their fear of failure**, we must create safe learning environments that recognise effort, build community and remove judgment. Finally, to inspire a love of **continuous learning**, it's critical to tap into students' interests and passions and foster a curiosity-driven approach to education that ignites their desire to explore and discover.

Beyond teaching adaptability, it is important to embed an **enterepreneurial** mindset from an early age. Entrepreneurs think differently because they approach work and business in a more creative way, often asking provocative questions. Their approach is not necessarily managerial or strategic – they believe they can impact the future and that it can be substantially shaped by their actions. The world is set to become more entrepreneurial than ever. That's down to a confluence of factors, such as young people seeing that traditional forms of higher education and climbing a corporate ladder aren't recipes for career success or happiness, and information on how to start a business is freely available.

The connection between having a business idea and creating jobs is weaker than ever. New businesses don't even need traditional employees anymore. Gig economy platforms and AI mean a lot of businesses can still grow for a long period without requiring full-time staff. At the time of writing, Open AI's Dall-E 2 shows the potential for marketing collateral to be created almost at the speed of thought.

Hadi Partovi, *CEO*
Code.org

(Note: This is not a contribution from Hadi. Permission has been granted to republish his LinkedIn post regarding the ban of ChatGPT in some schools.)

Schools banning ChatGPT?

Instead of banning technology, here's how schools can adjust to the reality of generative AI.

As an example, consider a high school history class, and a typical assignment: to read a book, and write an essay.

Whether we like it or not, AI can already write a pretty good essay in 10 seconds. And soon AI will include references and better fact-checking, and it will be built into Microsoft Word and Google Docs. Students will undoubtedly use this to 'cheat'.

First, let's stop thinking of this as 'cheating'. The learning objectives of school must evolve, and so must the assessments and assignments.

Let's stop measuring students based on what they produce all by themselves, let's not ban them from using the best tools on the internet, let's not ban them from working together. Every career requires the exact opposite skills: digital fluency and collaboration.

But we still want students to learn lessons from history, to think critically, and to communicate their insights. Instead of an essay, the history assignment could be to prepare for a debate, as a team.

Debate prep can include reading the book, using the internet, or even AI. Students would need to adapt to technology's strengths and weaknesses, learn to navigate misinformation, work together, and prepare to debate both sides of any argument.

A live debate won't test writing skills like an essay would, but it will test students' ability to research, think critically, collaborate, and communicate effectively. In an age of AI, aren't these more relevant skills?

And because teams wouldn't know which side of a debate they'll be assigned to, they would need to prepare for both sides – a skill that even us adults could benefit from in today's polarized world.

This example doesn't answer all questions about AI in education, but it suggests how things could evolve. Evolution will be

necessary in almost all subjects — not only changing how we teach, but also what we teach, what we measure.

Change isn't easy, but it's part of the human story. Students no longer use an abacus in math class, they use calculators. And they use grammar and spell-check software which is built-in to their word processor. Banning AI in schools will be a futile game of cat and mouse. Let's evolve and prepare students for a new era.

The future for entrepreneurship is bright because the conditions are right. Many businesses can start with a laptop and an internet connection. Location independence is already the watchword of digital nomads. They know it's not necessary to have a permanent office in a major city, instead turning towards co-working spaces wherever they happen to be. It's not just romantic notions of travel either. Better connectivity is having a positive impact on developing more rural and previously disconnected regional businesses too. It is also enabling access to a global market for sales and sourcing suppliers.

With so many back-office jobs being automated, there will simply be fewer traditional jobs available. With less traditional options available, it's inevitable that future generations will need to continue the work of Gen Z – the most entrepreneurial generation yet

– in creating niche products and services we haven't begun to think of yet. So, how do we equip them to do this? Well, what do Larry Page, Sergey Brin, Jeff Bezos, Anne Frank and Taylor Swift all have in common? The answer is they all had a Montessori education. I'm not advocating all parents should find a way to secure a Montessori education for their children, but there are some strong parallels between successful entrepreneurs and this style of teaching and learning that everyone could benefit from.

Learning from Montessori?

Montessori encourages children to co-develop their work plans each day with teachers. This happens from an early age, sometimes from as young as 5. Kindergarteners and entrepreneurs are similar in this respect. It also encourages responsible risk-taking. For example, children are encouraged to develop life skills from an early age, such as cutting up their own snacks (albeit with supervision). Not only do they get a chance to succeed, but also to see the consequences if it's done wrong. It's about helping children to do things for themselves. Teachers encourage children to explore their physical space and to experiment with materials that surround them. Entrepreneurs are similar in how they discover new ideas and find ways to manifest them to reality. By fostering curiosity, children get to become their authentic selves.

Another parallel with the entrepreneurial mindset is the approach to continual learning. In a Montessori classroom, learning doesn't stop, with fresh ideas being introduced constantly and children encouraged to follow up when their interest is piqued. Kindergartners and entrepreneurs enjoy their work because they feel passionate about it. Montessori encourages passion by allowing choice and exploration, which personalises the tasks and allows children to embrace their creativity because they have genuine autonomy over its direction. If a child feels driven by science and logic, Montessori teachers will help advance their knowledge in that domain. Ultimately, children leave feeling prepared for next-level education, but also equipped with important life skills, which enable them to follow their dreams and feel confident in doing so.

A Montessori education isn't for everyone's tastes or budget. But it does offer an inspiration point for all schools in terms of offering more training around entrepreneurial skills. At a minimum, schools need to help children understand the gig economy and techniques for better remote working. Any competencies that develop emotional intelligence are also welcome. For example, thriving in the gig economy world requires:

» Good communication skills
» A sense of self-motivation and direction
» Proving your trustworthiness (being reliable and consistent)
» Maintaining self-discipline
» Demonstrating initiative (proactively suggesting areas you can improve your contribution)
» Being flexible (a willingness to make life convenient for your boss (the person with the money to pay your price))
» Self-efficacy (believing in your capacity to deliver on agreed outcomes)

Activities that help students to develop such socio-emotional learning (SEL) skills are vital. For example, activities that involve a team planning a school event, creating a website and managing a social media presence around it, show students how the project-based work requires the co-ordination of a number of moving parts. There are even simulation resources available to support students to develop their SEL skills together. Take a look at 'STUKENT', which helps school-age students to explore marketing, social media for business and even offers real interactions with experts in different business fields.

Digital nomad millennials with young children are even rethinking the concept of school itself. Step forward, 'Worldschooling':

Nikolaj Astrup Madsen

Founder of Worldschooling.com

Remote work has been growing for many years, slowly becoming a bigger and bigger trend, with the growth increasing because of Covid. Digital nomads have gone from a small subculture to something available for a lot more people around the world.

At the same time, you see a growth in alternatives to school. The school system is in many ways built for the industrial age, and with the progress in opportunities, globalization and technology, simple school reform is not enough and more and more people are choosing to unschool or homeschool.

From this trend, a small sub trend has emerged: World-schooling. The idea of unschooling your kids while you are living nomadically, learning through experiencing the world. Small communities around this trend are evolving as events, meetups and online groups.

These huge shifts in how people decide to structure their life and the fact that over the last many centuries we have gone from living in communities to living in small nuclear family silos are opening up new ways to live.

That is why we are trying to build a traveling village. 20 families

traveling together, having communal meals and unschooling experiences for the kids. Combining what has worked for ages (being committed to a community, eating together) with the possibilities of the new world (remote work, full-time traveling, unschooling).

Digital Wellness: An evolved Approach to Digital Life?

With so much of our lives being lived online, what's a healthy approach to our digital lives? Notifications mean distraction, burnout is on the rise and the pandemic surfaced the idea of 'Zoom fatigue'. Certainly, remote working comes with its unique set of pressures and sometimes a sense of being trapped in the online space.

Much of the current thinking around solving these challenges involves some degree of unplugging from technology. Taking more breaks, removing unproductive apps, limiting time spent in front of screens – all are forms of abstinence and, as I've already touched on, worked for me.

However, some researchers are looking for a new path – one which seeks to make technology part of a happy life. In 2020, the Digital Wellness Institute was formed by Amy Blankson and Tyler Rice. Its purpose is 'to help humans thrive in the digital era'. Instead of viewing technology in terms of addiction or detoxing, it aims for something truly positive: **digital flourishing!**

In their own words, being 'digitally well' enables people to:

- Find focus and flow in work
- Live in harmony with both their physical and digital environments
- Connect in meaningful ways with others
- Enjoy strong relationships online and offline
- Build healthy physical and digital practices
- Embrace mindfulness and self-care through intentional technology use
- Understand how to manage their digital data and privacy
- Contribute to a positive digital community in their networks

When we focus on the positives of how technology can enhance our lives, we pursue digital wellness in pragmatic and creative ways, which is far more nuanced than online abstinence.

The Digital Wellness Institute sees digital wellness through a spectrum of experience:

- Digital Detox
- Digital Minimalism
- **Digital Flourishing**
- Technology Overuse
- Digital Addition

Optimising our lives for digital flourishing requires us to take a holistic approach to areas we want to improve, such as:

Addressing our physical and digital environment

We need to organise our environment. Setting up for success means putting in place your digital boundaries, and then communicating them clearly to family and work colleagues.

Sorry. Wednesday and Friday afternoons are deep work time.

That could mean restricting communication about work to specific times of the week. It could even mean only handling work-related tasks in specific locations; for example, never checking work emails at home, unless you're remote working. To avoid ambiguity, you could post your list of boundaries where they can easily be seen by colleagues and family.

Communication – a blessing and a curse!
Our email, messaging apps and social media amplify our opportunities for interacting with friends and family. It also curses us with new challenges.

For example, have you been at a res- taurant with a colleague? You might have been 'phubbed' (phone-snubbed) when they pick up their phone to check a message, even though you were dis- cussing an important work matter. It's poor etiquette.

You could make a joke out of it next time it happens – 'I'm feeling phubbed by you' – then explain what you mean. If you then do it yourself, it's entirely legitimate for them to hold you accountable as well. Many people – and some places – invite people to put phones face-down to give full attention back to their companions.

Optimising for productivity

Being productive means minimising those perpetual distractions. When we're optimised, we find more focus and a better work–life balance. It only takes a few seconds to read a WhatsApp message, but according to Gloria Mark of the University of California, it takes nearly twenty-five minutes to return to our original task. Turn off any automated notifications, like news alerts. Better yet, schedule all notifications to arrive at pre-specified times.

Maintaining good digital citizenship
We need to understand how our online com- munications can affect others, particularly in our increasingly diverse and inclusive world. For exam- ple, I choose not to engage in debate online as, for me personally, it's too easy to have my ideas misconstrued or misunderstood. With so much information available, our critical-thinking skills are

127

essential in deciding whether online information is truthful, biased or patently false.

Gaining control of your digital footprint

Taking time to understand data privacy and its implications is critical for ourselves and wider society. It's well worth gaining insight into your online footprint. A simple Google search on your name will show what information is visible publicly. If you deem it detrimental to your life, consider trying your best to remove it altogether. After all, why sacrifice your chances at a dream job for the sake of a drunken night-out picture!

General physical health

Extra screen time can lead to increased neck pain and back ache for many. It's even spawned a new phrase: 'tech neck'. If you work at a desk, especially at home, keep your screen at eye-level. Better yet,

consider a standing desk. Anything that avoids hunching and squinting helps us physically.

Quality not quantity in online relationships

There's a theoretical limit on the number of meaningful relationships a person can maintain. 'Dunbar's number' stipulates that a human can maintain a maximum of 150 'stable relationships'. Having 1,000 friends on your social network of choice isn't about friendship, they are acquaintances. There's also a clear distinction between 'followers' (typically one-way) and 'friends' (two-way). Our social media interactions can often lead to feelings of low self-esteem, particularly when 'relationships' are shallow or ephemeral. Maximise the value of your online connections by utilising advanced settings. How about creating a VIP list for your close friends, so only their updates are displayed when you check in. This reduces the likelihood of spending excessive time scrolling through negativity. If certain individuals or groups no longer bring value to your life, unfollow them or move them to secondary feeds.

Greater understanding though the 'quantified self'

The 'quantified self' means understanding yourself better, thanks to the data we obtain through technology. It's about using sensors through wearables (such as an Apple Watch) and recording that data in applications to optimise your health and performance. I found this approach personally helpful in losing weight after the Covid-19 lockdown. My 'Noom' app recorded daily footsteps via the phone and daily weigh-ins were recorded automatically from my IoT-enabled scales. I manually entered food intake and exercise. Through quantifying my activity, food and water, it helped me remain mindful and reach my weight-loss goal effortlessly.

Quantified self applications empower you to track and make sense of the data you create each day. You can try by starting something simple like your daily step count. Chances are your smartphone can record this automatically. Make a series of goals for yourself and celebrate each one when you achieve it.

These are a few basic steps you can take to boost your own digital wellness. If it piques your curiosity, do check out the Digital Wellness Institute for further resources.

Technology is ever-present in our lives and invaluable when we use it in a healthy way. But we needn't be a slave to it. With a few simple steps, we can become digital flourishers as opposed to getting lost in distraction. Through enhancing our digital wellness, we get to use technology for our own higher purpose and shape our positive future through the actions we take right now.

LIFE SHIFTS – HACKER HINTS

The following questions serve as hints for concepts you might want to ponder further to get future-ready.

Smart cities for a brighter future

Questions to ask yourself:

» Is it important for you to drive conversations about your locality and who it's designed for?

» What meaningful questions can you consider about green buildings and smart infrastructure that will serve you and your community?

» What steps can you take to help shape the positive future of your locality and promote inclusive design?

Rethinking education for the age of AI

Questions to ask yourself:

» Does your child's education include a focus on preparing them for the age of AI?

» How could education become more interdisciplinary and holistic?

» Does your child's school include a focus on developing an entrepreneurial mindset from an early age?

» How can AI technology be used to assist in learning, and why should schools embrace it?

» Does your child's education use AI technology to assist in their learning?

» How should learning objectives and assessments change to better prepare children for the age of AI?

The biotechnology revolution: what lies ahead

Questions to ask yourself:

» How do you feel about personalised medicine?

» Do you have a basic understanding of the ethical concerns arising from the use of epigenetics, such as gene editing in living creatures and human neuroenhancement?

» Do the opportunities arising from the human longevity industry interest you?

» Can you see how the biotechnology revolution would impact economies and societies? Are you concerned?

The holistic approach to digital wellness: achieving digital flourishing

Questions to ask yourself:

» How could you optimise your physical and digital environments to enhance your mental health and wellbeing?

» What steps could you take to practice good digital citizenship and control your digital footprint?

» In what ways could you maintain good physical health while using technology?

» How could you optimise your productivity in a way that supports your overall mental health and wellbeing?

» How could you view technology as a positive tool for enhancing your life, rather than just a source of distraction or stress?

» What concrete steps could you take to achieve 'digital flourishing' in your life?

THE NEXT FRONTIER

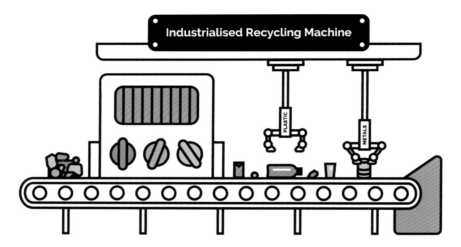

It seems fitting to end this exploration of the future where we started, with a laser lens on tech. Although, it's not really a looping back, as technological innovation has been the thread running throughout the whole book, as it will be the thread that runs through all of our lives moving forward. Nevertheless, I wanted to finish by moving on from explaining foundational tech to envisioning its implementation in our everyday existence.

GOING WHERE NO MACHINE
HAS GONE BEFORE

AI-assisted robotics are already transforming the world of manufacturing through wide-scale automation. As progress moves ahead, these machines will perform more sophisticated tasks and with less human intervention. In 2019, the Okuma corporation completed its Dream Site 3 Smart Factory in Kani, Japan. The company fuses AI, robotics, Industrial Internet of Things (IIoT) and knowhow to create manufacturing facilities that reduce lead times by up to 50%. The resultant lower operational and employee costs translate to lower costs for consumers.

This is just one example, it's not far off that we'll also see more AI and robots working alongside humans, too. Forecasts from market advisory firm ABI Research estimate the market for cobots to grow thirteen times its size from 2021–30. These robotic workers, known as 'cobots', will assist rather than replace their human counterparts. They are particularly suited to repetitive tasks such as lifting, picking and packing, which can be physically harmful to human workers. They will certainly improve efficiency and hopefully happiness for their human counterparts. In this way they will free us from the drudgery or responsibilities we don't really want. But more than that, they can be life-saving too.

Science fiction often portrays AI as being a destroyer or enslaver of human beings. Indeed, the entire *Terminator* franchise is based on that premise. But some AI developments are entirely centred around machines putting themselves in harm's way so humans don't have to.

Machines and humans already work together in the field of warfare. But in more everyday contexts, we're already beginning to see AI step into the fray; for example, in the world of firefighting. The Suppression Difficulty Index (SDI) is one of a number of analytical tools Dunn and other firefighting technology experts are building to bring the latest in machine learning, big data and forecasting to the world of firefighting. During the 2020 wildfires in northern California, firefighters received emails letting them know where their efforts would be most effective (and where not to bother).

In more mundane contexts, we've already looked in brief at how AI is forcing the job market to evolve. Its impact will change the way people do their jobs. Take the world of civil engineering, for example. AI will remove tedium by preparing survey data and laying the groundwork for new construction sites by automating the use of Computer Assisted Design (CAD). Civil engineers will have more time for creative design, optimisation and time with their clients to ensure they are happy.

AI and Creativity

What happens when AI meets culture? In 2016, a new painting in the style of Rembrandt, 'the Next Rembrandt', was designed by ANI and realised by a 3D printer, over three centuries after the painter himself died. To create it, 346 paintings were analysed, pixel by pixel. This formed the foundation of an algorithm designed to mimic the style of the artist himself. Many

art experts were amazed at the detail and accuracy of the brush strokes recreated by the 3D printer.

But... who's the creator here? Is it the company that designed the project? The engineers? The algorithm? Or, with all the data ultimately provided by Rembrandt, is it the great man himself? Under these circumstances, is copyright even attributable?

As AI learns to create art, we'll need a new definition for the words 'the artist'. Machine-originated creativity will need to acknowledge its influences, the underlying algorithms and the 'actuating' technology (such as a 3D printer or musical instruments) that produced the work itself. There's a crucial knock-on effect at play, too. Only

through effective rights attribution and artist remuneration can we avoid creative exploitation and continue to offer quality jobs in the cultural sector. This is just one example of how AI is beginning to change (or distort) the way we see the world, others are more insidious.

AI: Faking It and Making It

AI systems are becoming excellent at creating fake images, videos, conversations and all manner of content. Some of the best 'deep fakes' (synthetic media in which a person, object or location is digitally altered so they appear to be doing/saying/being something that is not reality) are hard to tell apart from the real thing.

Even if it's not a deep fake in terms of a visual representation, the proliferation of 'bots' that pose as people is a worrying trend. It's widely agreed that automated 'bots' played a significant part in securing the presidency of Donald Trump during the 2016 US elections. Bots are becoming more effective at spreading lies (or 'alternative facts' as they have also come to be called), amplifying untruths and just getting ideas into our heads through manipulating the algorithms that underpin the social networks we use everyday.

Criminals and state actors are using fake media to alter the perception of those to whom they wish

SURRENDER NOW!

to do harm. At the time of writing, Russian president Vladimir Putin has ordered an invasion of Ukraine by Russian armed forces previously concentrated along the two countries' shared border. In March 2022, 'Meta' (formerly Facebook) removed a fake video depicting Ukrainian president Volodymyr Zelenksy ordering his troops to surrender. Fortunately, the Ukrainian government and social media companies had learned lessons from previous instances and were prepared for this form of parallel information war. However, you can easily see the potential for a few malicious groups to spread false claims in this way and dramatically change public opinion in situations that might attract less attention. For example, these technologies could be easily used to ruin the reputation of a business by one of its competitors. At a more micro level, the world simply isn't prepared for AI being unleashed on unprotected people.

AI and Daily Life

As human lifespan extends and AI becomes more sophisticated, machines will support and augment our lives in increasingly sophisticated ways. The stilted Q&A we have with our smart speakers will give way to natural conversations with our virtual assistants that could know us better than we know ourselves. Through our dialogue and the data breadcrumbs we leave in our digital world, it will even get to understand our aspirations, life goals, limitations and obligations.

It will start to anticipate our near-future needs without being asked. Imagine an extreme weather event, such as a storm: school is can-

Your biometric information tells me you need cheering up. So, i've selected your favourite film Ghostbusters for your evening viewing.

celled and your planned visit to the office must be postponed so you can stay home. Your holographic voice assistant automatically asks if your meetings can be scheduled for the following day. Your entertainment system suggests appropriate films to watch or articles to read. The possibilities are limitless and an interactive voice initiates a conversation in a way that touching a screen cannot.

As we have already explored throughout this book, there will be many benefits and challenges of living alongside increasingly sophisticated machines. They will make our lives more convenient and efficient, but is this necessarily a good thing? We'll discover that there are costs to convenience. Ultimately, it will require us to mindfully navigate a life alongside machines in order that we don't become run by them. As AI grows in sophistication across real-world environments, it will need proper control mechanisms and strong ethical guidelines in place to benefit not hurt us. Without proper control, it could be the most destructive one since the invention of the machine gun.

WHO IS CONTROLLING WHO?: ETHICS AND THE DANGERS OF AI

There are so many issues that abound with the augmentation of our existence by AI and other tech, including a host of ethical considerations. The following areas of consideration are not exhaustive, and what's inevitable is that, as the technology develops, we'll become aware of others that we hadn't previously thought of.

Gender Bias

Try typing the word 'CEO' into a search engine image search. How many women do you see?

Try the same exercise for 'schoolgirl'. Do you see a series of young women in sexualised outfits? Now try the same for 'schoolboy'. The vast majority of results will be schoolboys in uniform.

The gender bias reflected in these results isn't a reflection of a sexist AI. It's much deeper than that. Such results are based on historical data that represent the deep stereotypes we have across society.

The insight we can draw from this is that our AI-fuelled search algorithms are far from neutral. They process results from big data, which in turn reflects all the biases we exhibit in society, giving the highest ranking to results most clicked by users and thus amplifying their preferences.

Not replicating gender bias in the digital world is so important that UNESCO has even published a legal document around the ethics of AI. Fairness and non-discrimination are central themes.

Autonomous Vehicles

Fully autonomous vehicles use a variety of sensors to understand their environment, and then drive themselves. To do so requires processing massive amounts of data, which is then processed by the vehicle's driving system. To be safe for humans, autonomous vehicles need significant training data in order to be capable of handling any real-world situation they find themselves in.

The ethics of autonomous vehicles has been covered in academic enquiry before, indeed long before autonomy on the roads ever existed. The 'trolley problem', first posed in 1967, is a thought experiment that highlights the complexities of decision-making where human life is at stake. In the Switch situation, a runaway trolley is hurtling down a track and will run into and kill five workmen unless an observer flips a switch. If the worker flips the switch, the trolley will divert down a sidetrack, where it will only kill one workman. Neither outcome is a good one, but the observer has the power to change it. The obvious ethical challenge is from the point of view of the sixth workman: what right does the observer have to kill the sixth workman? What right does society have to give the observer a moral imperative which will demonstrably cost someone their life?

such a grave decision lie? During the development and testing stages of automotive design, it undoubtedly lies with the manufacturer. However, the line blurs once these vehicles become fully commercialised. Expect to see significant legal precedent being created as insurers attempt to pass the buck and ethicists wrestle with the many unanswered questions.

Let's bring this dilemma up to date with self-driving cars. Let's suppose that the braking system has failed and the car is hurtling towards a grandmother and child. The system only has time to veer slightly, with the balance of probability suggesting that one, rather than both, will be killed. Which of them dies? Is there even a single answer?

Unlike the trolley experiment, it's now a machine that must make a life-or-death decision. Where does the ultimate responsibility for

Check out MIT's 'Moral Machine' for more thought experiments about the ethics of AI: **www.moralmachine.net**

FUTURE HACKERS

When considering the dangers of intelligent AI, the science-fiction writer Isaac Asimov is regularly cited. In 1942, he wrote the **three laws of robotics**. They are as follows:

First Law
A robot may not injure a human being or, through inaction, allow a human being to come to harm.

Second Law
A robot must obey the orders given it by human beings except where such orders would conflict with the First Law.

Third Law
A robot must protect its own existence as long as such protection does not conflict with the First or Second Law.

While originally conceived as a set of organising principles for his fiction, they have also had a significant impact on the ethics of AI. The key idea is that humans need to build in protective mechanisms to ensure that our sophisticated machine servants don't ultimately cause us harm.

I don't think our short- or medium-term futures herald us participating in scenes from *The Matrix*, *I, Robot* or *Terminator*. The dangers are more subtle than that. We should be aware of what these are and how we can counteract them. Our focus should be on how advances in AI technologies impact what it means to be human, to be productive and to exercise our free will.

The **Pew Research Centre** cites five major concerns with increasingly sophisticated machines running our lives:

1. **Loss of human agency:**
We experience a loss of control over our lives.

For example, our virtual assistants could become our bosses. It's already happening. Look to food delivery services, such as Uber Eats. Drivers and riders are managed by algorithms, with deadlines to meet and schedules to adhere to. In this context, humans are managed, and expectations of their performance set, by machines.

You must m
the deadline
you're fire

2. Abuse of our data:

Our digital breadcrumbs are everywhere and surveillance in complex systems is designed for profit or exercising power.

China's Social Credit System is an example of surveillance to some degree gone rogue. Citizens are ranked based on 'social credit', as determined by the Communist Party. Bad driv-

ing, debt or playing too much on video games could all lead you to being banned from taking flights or having your internet speed throttled. What happens if a version of this were to extend to our workplaces or, worse still, society at large?

3. Job losses:

As demonstrated in the chapter the Future of Work, some new jobs will emerge, but many will be lost.

As more of our work is automated by machines, we could see increased inequality and social upheaval, with more populist uprisings. Governments around the world will need to seriously consider ways of providing income and a sense of purpose for their citizens.

4. Dependence lock-in:

A reduction of our cognitive, social and survival skills

The hope is that AI would augment our human capabilities, but it could easily go the other way. The more we rely on machines, the harder it becomes to think for ourselves. I'll always remember how my primary school teachers insisted we learn arithmetic and not rely on calculators. That might turn out to have been a good thing!

5. Anarchy and mayhem:

More autonomous weapons, cyber-crime and weaponised information.

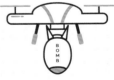

As new conflict sparks around the world, would we see an increased loss of life due to autonomous weapons and other unintended consequences of automations? Sophisticated propaganda is already being used to destabilise populations. Cybercriminals could use sophisticated tools which distance them from the crimes they perpetrate on whole economic systems.

So, how do we go about solving these problems? Firstly, we must focus on global good and improve collaboration across borders and between different stakeholder groups. Second, a values-based system must be developed to ensure that AI is directed towards promoting the common good. Finally, it is crucial to prioritise people by altering economic and political systems to help them keep pace with the rapid advancements in technology. In short, our AI systems must address our **humanness**; that which makes us human. It must include our ability to understand and care for others, show kindness and have a moral compass. The rules we create for AI must take these special human qualities into account, so that it can be deployed in a way that benefits everyone.

The central debate is over human autonomy and **agency** in the world. Operating in the digital world means some sacrifice to our independence, privacy and choice – but how much?

Good morning. Your ACMECORP Oatmeal Breakfast bar is ready to eat.

To stay competitive, to be social and entertained, how much control do we cede to tech that can serve these goals? Right now, the content served to you on Facebook or Netflix adapts itself to your perceived interests. Machines attempt to avoid choice overload (and to keep us profitably engaged) by substituting our decision-making with their algorithmic predictions. I think we need systems that support rather than replace our decision-making. If we're not mindful, even our breakfast choice could be dictated by a machine that maximises our efficiency and the supplier's profit rather than our wellbeing.

Our direction-finding mapping applications prize the fastest route. How about an app that takes us on the most beautiful route rather than the quickest? Or a communications application that deepens the relationships with our most treasured connections as opposed to maximising the number of people we connect with? Technology that's truly people-centred isn't based on maximising the profits of its creators. Rather, it would constantly anticipate and ask what's most important to us and how would we prefer to use our time in any given moment. Efficiency has its place, but not at the price of the satisfying moments that make life worth living!

As AI continues to advance, it's crucial that we stay mindful of its ethical implications. Ignoring them could lead to dire consequences. But can we trust organisations and governments to steer AI in a responsible direction? The answer is no. It's a conversation that demands participation from everyone: from the education system to the general public. By increasing awareness and encouraging dialogue, we can shape the future of AI in a way that maximises its benefits and minimises harm. Unfortunately, there will always be those looking to exploit AI for personal gain. So, it's important for all of us to stay vigilant, ask questions and educate ourselves about AI's impact on our lives. This impact will only continue to grow, and it's up to us to be prepared for it.

RELATING TO ROBOTS

Throughout this book we've explored how robots are becoming more widespread and have disrupted many industries. That's business, but in our personal lives can they combat loneliness and help us become happier?

If dogs are a person's best friend, then the pandemic might have proved how robots are going to come a close second.

In Italy, after six doctors became infected with Covid-19, a hospital brought in ultraviolet disinfection robots to sanitise treatment and operating areas. The pandemic accelerated the application of robots to all sorts of situations in order to maintain social distancing and reduce infection risk.

But Covid-19 also showed how robots could provide emotional support, too. Researchers at the UK's Heriot-Watt University began a study in 2020 to address the resulting loneliness caused by isola-tion and social distancing. The study, titled 'Ambient Assisted Living', involved programming 'Pepper' robots to assist with household tasks in a 'smart flat lab'. At the time of writing, it wasn't possible to find publicly available results.

What's Love Got To Do With It?

'Sex dolls' were first used by sailors in the sixteenth century. Made from sewn cloth or old clothes, these could be considered crude predecessors to what's available now. But crude is an understatement compared to what could be around the corner.

In a world where more interaction happens online than offline, it's not hard to imagine how AI and robotics will combine for romance, love and intimacy. Our human–machine relationships are becoming richer, whether that's with our smart speakers or self-driving cars. Science fiction has explored the theme of love between humans and robots on several occasions, including the Oscar-nominated *Ex-Machina*, *Blade Runner*, *Westworld* and *Black Mirror*, all of which feature humans developing intense feelings of love for different forms of AI in avatar form.

So, step forward 'Robosexuals'. In *Love and Sex with Robots*, author David Levy suggests that one day love with robots will be as normal as with other human beings. He envisions combining AI and robotics for an answer to the problems some people find with intimacy. To do so meaningfully, these robots will need to sense their users. They'll need to analyse their users' emotions, then create appropriate emotional reactions and paralinguistic (gesture, expression, tone, etc.) cues of their own. That will require a high degree of emotional reasoning, too.

'To call me a sex robot is like calling a computer a calculator,' says Harmony X, the US$7,000 robot available right now from the market leader in realistic sex dolls, Realdoll. Founder Matt McMullen has ambitions to evolve his dolls so that they 'think' and learn what their partner wants – to be a full substitute for a real-world partner. Eventually he expects a doll to listen, remember and talk naturally, like an actual person would.

In the course of researching Robosexuality, I happened to discuss it with a friend in her early thirties. I'd half expected her to be judgemental and dismissive. It was surprising – to me – that she seemed ambiguous at worst, if not positive. 'A lot of my friends are finding it hard to meet men for meaningful relationships,' she said. 'A lot of the guys they meet are only up for one-night stands or, worse still, they get ghosted before even meeting up. Maybe robots are the answer.' I could tell that she was only half joking.

These conversations demonstrate that AI and robots raise real questions about how new ways of experiencing love could engage us in compelling and meaningful relationships, not just of the sexual variety. In some cases, they might be the only chance people have for a profound bond or a chance of satisfying the emotional needs of the elderly or socially challenged individuals. Once sufficiently sophisticated, they could be a real asset to society, providing companionship and care. AI researcher David Levy predicts that by 2050, romantic and sexual relationships with robots will become normalised and widely accepted. He also foresees that marriages between humans and robots will be legally recognised. The real question for me is how our interactions with machines for love and sex will impact our emotions and perceptions of the flesh-and-blood humans we otherwise choose to spend our time with.

Let's continue to remove any judgment from the equation. It's obvious that sophisticated robotics will change the way we behave, just as social media and innumerable other trends – from the telephone forward – have done.

That includes the nature of friendship, our willingness to help others and our concept of love. Well-known science fiction about robotics tends to focus on our relationships with robots themselves. In *2001: A Space Odyssey* we see the Hal 9000 planning to murder its human masters. In *Star Wars*, C-3PO and R2-D2 are useful team members in the rebel alliance's attempt to defeat the empire. Neither story explored the most relevant question to us today: how will AI and robotics change the way we humans relate to one another?

While both the telephone and internet enabled instant communication, they didn't change the fundamental tenets of how we viewed and valued each other, but they did accelerate and enable new forms of behaviour. What happens when AI and robotics go mainstream across the world's societies? Their capacity to understand our emotion, analyse it, and then synthesise responses that feed our ego has the potential to create a more profound shift in humanity. When they are deeply embedded in our lives, they could easily impact how kind, friendly or loving we are – especially with one another.

Even today, our simple interactions with AI could have consequences. Some parents are already concerned about how their children are interacting with digital assistants like Amazon's Echo device. They see their kids rudely yelling orders at these devices and are concerned that these behaviours could become normalised, impacting their children's human relationships. Sherry Turkle, an MIT expert on technology and society, believes that children who grow up being looked after by AI and robots might not 'acquire the equipment for empathic connection'. He reached that insight after seeing how his own son interacted with a toy robot.

At the most practical level, machines will impact our capacity for co-operation. Driving a car is a good example. We need to follow traffic lights and road signs to get to our destination safely and avoid accidents. But if self-driving cars become common, we won't have the chance to use our skills as much. And if we don't use them, they will get weaker. When humans drive, we also have to make tough decisions in case of an accident. With self-driving cars, we will lose some of our agency in the world. That's not necessarily a bad thing. Let's just be mindful it's happening.

Robots and Motherhood. The Ultimate Fusion of Humans and Machines?

In March 2022, scientists and researchers from Vermont University created the world's first 'Xenobot', a fusion of life and machines in a single entity. They took living cells from the heart and skin of a frog and then used supercomputer AI to configure it. While extremely crude, their applications could have profound applications in healthcare. With further development, there is hope the technology could evolve and form new nanotechnology for tackling tumours inside the human body. They would be equipped with their own food source and could even have the ability to reproduce.

While they could easily disrupt and transform healthcare and other industries, these biorobots open up a range of new concerns. If machines can fuse with biology and reproduce, what's to say they couldn't be used to reproduce humans in their entirety? If they can gestate a human embryo, would sex for human reproduction even be needed? In time, it could even be seen as too risky – yet another job 'best left to the robots'?!

These next frontiers of technology may thrill or terrify, depending on your comfort level with a machine-driven future. Either way, we're moving into realms that have previously been inhabited by the writers and dreamers of science fiction, and in order to thrive in this new paradigm, we have to focus on cementing and enriching our 'humanness' – the skills and attributes that ensure we won't cede all control to AI because we'll still want to learn and create new things, as well as love and protect one another.

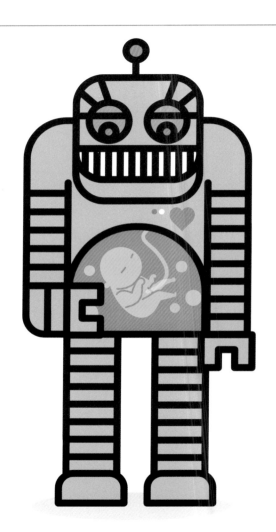

THE NEXT FRONTIER – HACKER HINTS

The following questions serve as hints for concepts you might want to ponder further to get future-ready.

Machines on the march

Questions to ask yourself:

» Is AI already changing your industry and your role within it?
» Could you imagine a situation where you find yourself working alongside a 'Cobot'?
» Have you considered the potential benefits and risks of AI to culture, particularly with regards to art and copyright?
» How can we ensure effective rights attribution and artist remuneration in the age of AI and automation, and why is this important for maintaining quality jobs in the cultural sector?

The ethics of AI: a revolution in need of regulation

Questions to ask yourself:

» How does AI impact your life in general?
» Do you understand gender and other biases in AI systems, and why it matters? Are you on guard for it?
» Where does responsibility lie in the case of an accident involving an autonomous vehicle?
» How can we remain aware of the dangers of AI and ensure that it is developed in a way that aligns with our values and priorities as a society?

The profound future question of human–robot relationships

Questions to ask yourself:

» How do you feel about the idea of robots being integrated into our daily lives, including in the workplace and as emotional support?
» Do you think romantic relationships with robots will become normal and widely accepted by 2050?
» What impact might human-robot relationships have on human-human relationships, and how might we address any potential negative effects?
» In what ways do you think AI and robotics will change the way we behave, including our friendships, willingness to help others, and concept of love?
» How do we ensure that robots and AI are developed and used in ways that align with our values and ethics, especially as they relate to human relationships and interactions?

Authors note: In the beginning of the book, I mentioned that I hope it'll help you have your own personal 'a-ha' moments. Now, the next contributor we have is seriously passionate about helping people understand themselves through self-enquiry. I think you're going to really enjoy what he has to share!

Piers Thurston
Quality of Mind founder
www.qualityofmind.biz

THE SECRET TO ALL CHANGE AND EVOLUTION

Technology, new norms on the speed of change, and ways of working are leading to wholesale societal change. The ability to evolve, adapt and even transform is only going to be needed more. So, what does that mean for individuals and their ability to change?

For change that is sustainable, self-perpetuated and truly relevant and valuable, understanding the human mind is crucial – going beyond just the knowledge and the intellectual adoption of concepts of both what we are, and how we believe human potential is realised.

So, what are we missing?: The power of realisation

Realisation is when one set of perceptions, mindsets and behaviours dissolves and new ones arise; it equips us with the resourcefulness, inspiration and actions to move forward. Post-realisation insights tend not to slip back to old ways, and there is obviousness about the new way. Just think about how we learn to ride a bike, knowing intellectually how balance works has no bearing on our ability to do it. And once it's 'clicked' for us we never forget (hence the familiar saying!).

The innocent mistake

There is a popular figure for organisational change – 70% of all change initiatives fail.

WHY? We either ignore the power of realisation or are innocently and invisibly going about harnessing the power of realisation in the wrong way:

» You can't force yourself or others to experience a realisation.
» Just informing or influencing people to change doesn't lead to realisation.
» We get too focused on the content of our realisations as opposed to respecting the infinite human capacity for them.
» In the context of organisational change, often people's psychologies are triggered into a contracted aperture (increased effort, or control, or fight or flight response) which makes them less open to realisation.

Yet we are all designed for realisation and change

Humans are perfectly designed and set up to change, they can't not. Small children are the best example: the amount of new pieces of information, behaviours and concepts they process is vast, and they do it without any effort.

Any of us can notice how realisation happens naturally and with obviousness in certain areas of our lives, and these are the areas where we have least self-identification and attachment. This leads us to the apparent paradox: if we are least open to realisation in the areas where we are most attached, how do we facilitate realisation where we need it most?

How to Harness the Power of Realisation

We need to unlearn (naturally via our own realisations) the beliefs we have about what we are, and how to get the best from the mind:

» We are addicted to thinking with normalised, busy minds. This is exaggerated in organisations, especially in times of change.

» In our attempts to manage change and personal development we miss the understanding of the mind and even the nature of what 'we are'. We are holding on too tight, trying to manage, control and grind our way through development – ignoring the fact that actually 'nature lives us' and it just appears that we have a sense of agency.

» Instead, we need to realise the natural intelligence in the system. Then the psychological interference we innocently and invisibly add to it, based on our belief that we are a limited, separate self that needs to seek security, wellbeing and success from events and circumstances, or from 'who we are' in the world.

Experiment for Yourself

Notice how change in your life has actually happened. Those minor or major shifts may have appeared to have come from some form of stimulus event or circumstance, but did they actually or is that just more of a post-rationalised piece of meaning made from the conceptual mind (the personal mind loves to try to understand 'why' something happened, but can be an unreliable narrator on it)?

So, consider for you how it has happened in your life so far – that piece of obviousness that arose, the thing that 'clicked', the inspiration to move forward, the persistence to focus on the journey not the result. They are all signs of a realised change.

We can't force or contrive that, despite our common attempts to reverse engineer realisation by finding a foolproof mental strategy or process. It arises in an embodied way, often tangential and conflated with external or internal events but never caused by them.

Spend a moment to separate out the correlation of how you think change happened to how it actually arose, and then experiment with the fact that realisation is available always as a capacity of the mind: 100% reliable; 95% unpredictable.

You never know, you might surprise yourself in what you realise.

Realisation: it is the most significant yet unrecognised and misunderstood leverage point for change.

CONCLUSION

If I had to draw together the many themes that are changing our lives at such a dramatic rate, and which we've looked at here, I'd like to convey two core realisations that have shaped how I perceive future hacking and readiness.

Recently, there's been a significant surge in public recognition and adoption of AI technology. From the text transformer 'ChatGPT' exploding onto the scene to the incredible displays of text-to-image creation using MidJourney and Stable Diffusion, these AI technologies are impressive but still demonstrate significant flaws.

It's unclear how far and how rapidly they'll continue to develop. However, their capabilities have the potential to rocket humanity into a new epoch. Ethical issues will have to be kept front-of-mind when defining the levels of agency we intend to give these advanced tools, or else we could face catastrophic consequences.

I can't offer greater clarity on how quickly these **specific*** AI models will or will not develop, but I offer three possible scenarios:

These AI models have reached the peak of their capacity:	We have incredible new tools that make our work more efficient. This scenario is unlikely to destroy many jobs.
These AI models are at the middle of their path to peak capacity:	We can expect some truly mind-blowing new tools in the near future which still require humans to operate them.
These AI models are only at the beginning of their peak capacity:	Everything is about to change – and fast. This scenario is similar to what we witnessed in the late 1990s, when the rise of online services directly caused an implosion of old business models.

*It is entirely possible that other AI models could arise and surpass these existing models.

Although I'm unsure about the rate at which these **specific** AI models will advance, I'm absolutely certain about their profound impact on our daily lives.

By exploring this new wave of AI-powered tools, you will be able to reap substantial benefits and improve your productivity. You have the option of using this increased productivity to either reclaim time for other more enjoyable activities, or to gain a competitive advantage in your profession or business. Ultimately, the decision is yours.

Regardless of which scenario plays out, my advice remains the same: get comfortable with the changes that advanced technology will bring and develop a new mindset to help navigate these changes successfully.

This brings me to my second key theme: I recommend developing your synthesising mindset; it will help connect the dots and allow you to find creative solutions to the challenges life throws at you. Practice active listening when conversing with others. Take the time to understand their perspectives and how those perspectives fit into the larger picture of your personal experience. Encouraging diverse perspectives helps us to avoid becoming narrow-minded.

Next, look for connections and patterns between seemingly unrelated pieces of information. Be open to new ideas and be willing to accept different points of view. Take time to reflect on your own thought processes, and don't be afraid of failure. Failure teaches us valuable lessons and helps us improve our problem-solving skills.

Finally, read widely. Diversify your reading materials to help you develop a broader perspective and see connections between different fields of knowledge. In short, developing a synthesising mindset will make you future-ready and help you handle challenges with creativity and confidence.

I hope this book has been helpful, and you feel well-equipped to 'hack the future'!

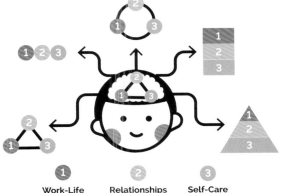

1 Work-Life Balance **2** Relationships **3** Self-Care

ACKNOWLEDGMENTS

I am deeply grateful to the following people, whose generous contributions made this book possible:

» My family, for their unwavering support and encouragement.
» Jo De Vries at Flint Publishing, for her expertise in editing and for patiently bringing structure to a stream of consciousness.
» Claire Hopkins at Flint Publishing, for her logistical support and for keeping everything on track.
» Nick Saalfeld from ModComms, for his expert sense-making and valuable writing advice.
» Caroline Hayward and Nikolina Miljush, for their invaluable assistance with research.
» Rita Ottolini from ModComms, for her outstanding work in designing and illustrating the entire book.
» David Wood, Chair of London Futurists, for his thoughtful and inspiring foreword.

Additionally, I am deeply grateful for the outstanding contributions of the following individuals:

» Anna Gudmundson, Dr Freija Van Duijne, Hadi Partovi, Henry Rose-Lee, Kay Vasey, Nikolaj Astrup Madsen, Piers Thurston, Russell Atkinson, Sharon O'Dea and Yewande Akinola, for their self-contained contributions.

» Angie DIY, Annie Sobremente, Caron Fassetta, Clara Lopez, Dalia Dannawi, David Norton, Djordje Devic, Dr Everisto Doria, Dr Jessica S. Dunn, Emma Pownall, Fanni Zoldos, Hardi Darweish, Jamal White, John O'Driscoll, Julie Lucca, Laurence Hollobon, Maria Franzoni, Mia Gemmecke, Paul Foley, Peter Cohen, Professor James Woudhuysen, Scott Addington, Stephen Welch, Virginie Derwent and Yildiz Atan, who provided me with inspiration, ideas and encouragement, even though they didn't always realise it.

FURTHER READING

AI Ethics by Mark Coeckelbergh, 2020, The MIT Press

Algorithms, Blockchain & Cryptocurrency by Gavin Brown and Richard Whittle, 2020, Emerald Publishing Limited

A New Kind of Diversity by Tim Elmore and John Maxwell, 2022, Maxwell Leadership

Apollo's Arrow: The Profound and Enduring Impact of Coronavirus on the Way We Live by Nicholas A. Christakis, 2020, Little Brown & Company

Elon Musk's Neuralink by Dr Christopher Braxton, 2022, Independently Published

Future Crimes by Marc Goodman, 2016, Corgi

Future Food (Kindle Edition) by Aaron Council & Michael Petch, 2015, Gyges 3D Presents

Genentech: The Beginnings of Biotech by Herbert Boyer, 2013, Chicago Press

Generation Alpha by Mark McCrindle, 2023, Hachette Australia

Into the Metaverse by Cathy Hackl, 2023, Bloomsbury Business

Leadership by Algorithm by David De Cremer, 2020, Harriman House Ltd

#Loneliness: The Virus of the Modern Age by Tony Jeton Selimi, 2016, Balboa Press

Multiple Intelligences by Howard Gardner, 2006, Basic Books

Smart Cities for Dummies by Jonathan Reichental, 2020, For Dummies

Super Intelligence by Nick Bostrom, 2014, Oxford University Press

Technology vs. Humanity by Gerd Leonhard, 2016, Fast Future Publishing

The Abolition of Ageing by David Wood, 2016, Delta Wisdom

The Age of Surveillance Capitalism by Shoshana Zuboff, 2020, Public Affairs

The Artist in the Machine: The World of AI-Powered Creativity by Arthur Miller, 2020, The MIT Press

The Future of the Professions by Richard and Daniel Susskind, 2020, Oxford University Press

The Gig Economy by Diane Mulcahy, 2016, AMACOM

The Infinite Retina by Robert Scoble and Irena Cronin, 2020, Packt Publishing

The Planet Remade: How Geoengineering Could Change the World by Oliver Morton, 2017, Princeton University Press

The Quantified Self by Deborah Lupton, 2016, Polity Press

The Technological Singularity by Murray Shanahan, 2015, MIT Press

Turned On: Science, Sex and Robots by Kate Devlin, 2018, Bloomsbury Sigma

Understand How to Rest and Recover in this "Always on" Society by Jessie Fields, 2022, Indepedently published

Zero Distance: Management in the Quantum Age by Danah Zohar, 2022, Palgrave Macmillan Singapore

Matt O'Neill
The Optimistic Futurist

Keynote speaker and author

Dedicated to creating a positive future for your organisation

Gives your audience inspiration, optimism and actionable insights for an exciting near-future

I speak at conferences and run bespoke seminars and workshops for leadership teams looking for practical, optimistic inspiration to develop new strategies for their organisations.

We'll ask: What can you do tomorrow that you're not doing today? And what difference can you hope to make?

Every event includes:

» Practical ideas, concepts and tools to implement afterwards in your own context.
» Bespoke visuals to bring ideas to life and communicate effectively from the boardroom to the shop floor.
» Easy to read cheat-sheets to keep, covering more detailed concepts.
» The option to connect with me on LinkedIn to follow up with discussions.

Are you ready to take your events to the next level? Well, guess what? You're in luck because I'm here and available for absolutely everything!

That's right, whether you're looking for an in-person presenter that'll knock your socks off, a virtual gathering that'll leave your guests buzzing, or even a mind-blowing metaverse experience, I'm your go-to optimistic futurist! So let's make your next event unforgettable and get ready to blow everyone's minds together!

futurist.matt

the optimistic futurist

Call now: +44 (0)20 7193 0104

Email: info@futuristmatt.com

For more information:
www.futuristmatt.com

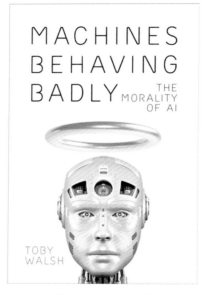